Cruising
The Microsoft® Network

Cruising Books

...ca Online 2.5

Visual Learning Guides

or Windows: The Visual Learning Guide

...ss for Windows 95: The Visual Learning Guide

! 2.0 for Windows: The Visual Learning Guide

el for the Mac: The Visual Learning Guide

...cel for Windows 95: The Visual Learning Guide

...ternet for Windows: America Online 2.5 Edition

Internet for Windows: The Microsoft Network Edition

PROCOMM PLUS for Windows: The Visual Learning Guide

PowerPoint for Windows 95: The Visual Learning Guide

Quicken 5 for Windows: The Visual Learning Guide

WinComm PRO: The Visual Learning Guide

Windows 3.1: The Visual Learning Guide

Windows 95: The Visual Learning Guide

WinFax PRO: The Visual Learning Guide

Word 6 for the Mac: The Visual Learning Guide

Word for Windows 6: The Visual Learning Guide

Word for Windows 95: The Visual Learning Guide

WordPerfect 6 for Windows: The Visual Learning Guide

WordPerfect 6.1 for Windows: The Visual Learning Guide

Upcoming Books!

Cruising CompuServe

Microsoft Works for Windows 95: The Visual Learning Guide

WinFax PRO 7 for Windows: The Visual Learning Guide

How to Order:

Individual orders and quantity discounts are available from the publisher, Prima Publishing, P.O. Box 1260BK, Rocklin, CA 95677-1260; (916) 632-4400. For quantity orders, include information on your letterhead concerning the intended use of the books and the number of books you wish to purchase.

Cruising
The Microsoft® Network

Grace Joely Beatty, Ph.D.

David C. Gardner, Ph.D.

David A. Sauer, M.S.

PRIMA PUBLISHING

Project Editor: Kelli Crump

If you have problems installing or running The Microsoft® Network contact Microsoft at (800) 386-5550 or (214) 776-2626. Prima Publishing cannot provide software support.

Prima Publishing and the authors have attempted throughout this book to distinguish proprietary trademarks from descriptive terms by following the capitalization style used by the manufacturer.

ISBN: 0-7615-0378-1
Library of Congress Catalog Card Number: 95-71603
96 97 98 99 AA 10 9 8 7 6 5 4 3 2 1
Printed in the United States of America

Acknowledgments

We are deeply indebted to reviewers around the country who gave so generously of their time to test every step in the manuscript. In addition to manuscript testing, Craig Patchett contributed significantly, writing many chapters.

We are personally and professionally delighted to work with everyone at Prima Publishing.

Linda Miles, technical editor; Suzanne Stone, copy editor; Marian Hartsough, interior layout; Emily Glossbrenner, indexer; and Paul Page, cover design, contributed immensely to the final product.

Bill Gladstone and Matt Wagner of Waterside Productions created the idea for this series. Their faith in us has never wavered.

Joseph and Shirley Beatty made this series possible. We can never repay them

Asher Shapiro has always been there when we needed him.

Paula Gardner Capaldo and David Capaldo have been terrific. Thanks, Joshua and Jessica, for being such wonderful kids! Our project humorist, Mike Bumgardner, always came through when we needed a boost!

Thanks again to Cyrus and Jemmie for their selfless assistance.

We could not have met the deadlines without the technical support of Ray Holder, our electrical genius, Diana M. Balelo, Frank E. Straw, Daniel W. Terhark and Martin J. O'Keefe of Computer Service & Maintenance, our computer wizards.

Contents at a Glance

Customize Your Learning

Prima's Cruising books are not like any other computer books you have ever seen. They are based on our years in the classroom, our corporate consulting, and our research at Boston University on the best ways to teach technical information to non-technical learners. Most importantly, this series is based on the feedback of a panel of reviewers from across the country who range in computer knowledge from "panicked at the thought" to "sophisticated."

This is not an everything-you've-ever-wanted-to-know-about-The Microsoft® Network book. It is designed and written to let you quickly become familiar with the basics of using the network, while giving you an introduction to its more popular resources. In addition, you will learn several advanced functions and techniques effortlessly, giving you added confidence and skill for all your computer-related activities.

Each chapter is illustrated with color screens to guide you through every task. The combination of screens, step-by-step instructions, and pointers makes it impossible for you to get lost or confused as you follow along on your own computer. You can either work through from beginning to end or skip around to master the skills you need. Our reviewers claim that this format makes it "really easy" for anyone to find his or her way around The Microsoft Network quickly.

We truly hope you'll enjoy using this book and The Microsoft Network. Let us know how you feel about our book and whether there are any changes or improvements we can make. You can contact us through Prima Publishing at 3875 Atherton Road, Rocklin, CA 95765 or send us an e-mail letter. Our address is gbgroup@msn.com. Thanks for buying the book. Enjoy!

David, Joely, and David

The Microsoft Network

Part I: Setting Up The Microsoft Network

Installing The Microsoft Network and Exchange

You have the option of installing The Microsoft Network when you install Windows 95. Microsoft Exchange is the electronic mail program used by The Microsoft Network (MSN). If you installed MSN, Exchange will also have been installed. If you did not install MSN, you can do it now. You need a major credit card to sign up for the network. In this chapter you will do the following:

✔ Install The Microsoft Network
✔ Set up the Exchange Inbox for your e-mail
✔ Store your Member ID and Password for signing on more easily

INSTALLING MSN

In this section we assume that you have not installed MSN. If you installed it, but haven't tried to sign on to the network yet, skip to the next section, titled "Getting Connected." Your screen may have different icons and/or folders from the ones shown here.

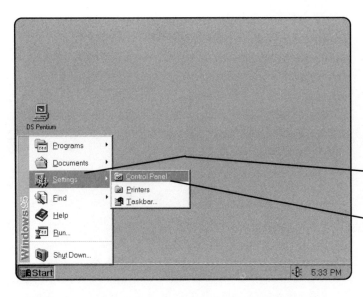

1. **Get** the **CD or disks** that you used to install Windows 95. You will need to have them on hand to install MSN.

2. **Click** on **Start** on the taskbar. The Start menu will appear.

3. **Click** on **Settings**. Another menu will appear.

4. **Click** on **Control Panel**. The Control Panel window will appear.

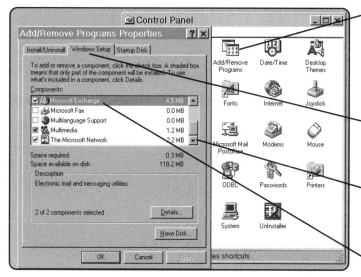

5. **Click twice** on the **Add/Remove Programs icon**. The Add/Remove Programs Properties dialog box will appear.

6. **Click** on the **Windows Setup tab**. The Windows setup page will appear.

7. **Click repeatedly** on the ▼ to scroll to the bottom of the list of choices.

8. **Click twice** on Microsoft Exchange. The Microsoft Exchange dialog box will appear.

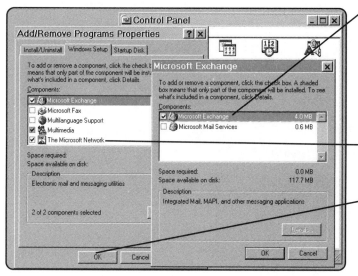

9. **Click** on **Microsoft Exchange** to place a ✔ next to it.

10. **Click** on **OK**. The dialog box will close.

11. **Click** on **The Microsoft Network** to place a ✔ by it.

12. **Click** on **OK**. You will be prompted to insert the CD or disk you used to install Windows 95.

Follow any directions that appear on your screen. When installation is complete, the Add/Remove Programs Properties dialog box will close. Click on the Close button (⊠) to close the Control Panel window.

GETTING CONNECTED

Once the programs for The Microsoft Network and Exchange are installed, their icons will appear on your desktop. (If the Control Panel window is still open, click on the Close button on its title bar to close it.) Do not rename, delete, or move these icons.

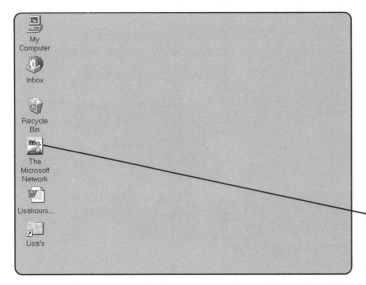

Because of Windows 95 programming, they must be on your desktop and recognizable to the operating system for the MSN connection and e-mail to work properly. If they are ever deleted, you will have to uninstall and reinstall MSN and Microsoft Exchange for the programs to work again.

1. **Click twice** on **The Microsoft Network icon**. A Microsoft Network dialog box will appear.

2. **Click** on **OK**. Another Microsoft Network dialog box will appear.

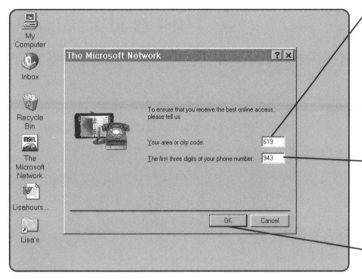

3. **Type** your **Area Code** in the upper box and **press** the **Tab key**. (If you entered your telephone number when you installed Windows 95, both of the boxes will already have your numbers in them.)

4. **Type** your **local exchange number** (the first three digits of your phone number) in the lower box.

5. **Click** on **OK**. The Calling dialog box will appear.

Making Contact

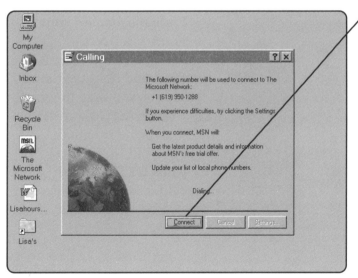

1. **Click** on **Connect**.

The progress of your first call to the network will be shown in this dialog box. The program will dial into the network, download an updated list of telephone numbers, and disconnect. After the call disconnects, another Microsoft Network dialog box will appear.

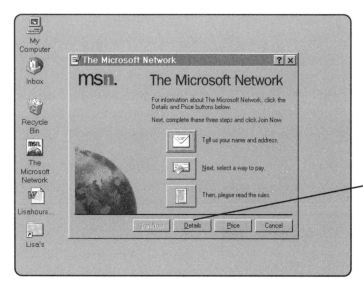

Doing the Paperwork

Now you have some information to read and a few electronic forms to fill out and send to the network.

1. Click on **Details**. Another Microsoft Network dialog box will appear.

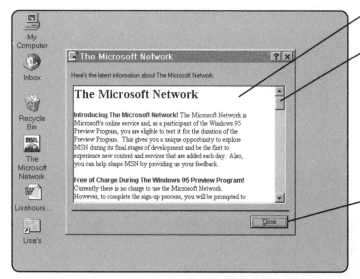

2. Read the **information**.

3. Place the **mouse arrow** over the scroll box.

4. Press and hold the **mouse button** as you **drag** the scroll box down the bar to read the rest of the information.

5. Click on **Close**. The previous Microsoft Network dialog box will reappear.

6. Repeat steps 1–5, clicking on the button marked "Price" to read that information.

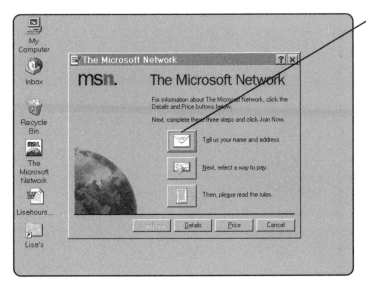

7. **Click** on the **icon** next to "Tell us your name and address." Another Microsoft Network dialog box will appear.

Filling in the Blanks

1. **Type** your **first name** and **press** the **Tab key**. The cursor will move to the next box.

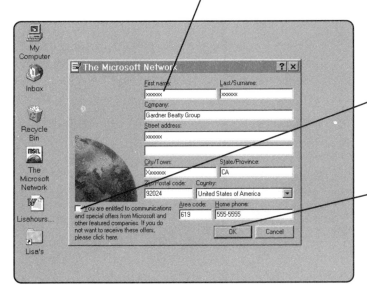

2. **Continue** in this way until you have filled in all of the boxes.

3. **Click** on **this box** to place a ✔ in it if you do not wish to receive advertising mail related to the network.

4. **Click** on **OK**. The previous Microsoft Network dialog box will reappear.

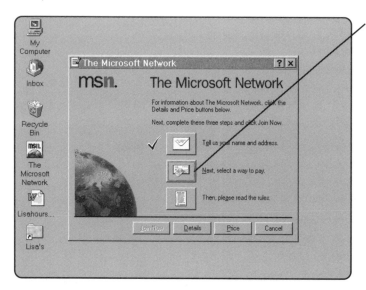

5. **Click** on the **icon** beside "Next, select a way to pay." Another Microsoft Network dialog box will appear.

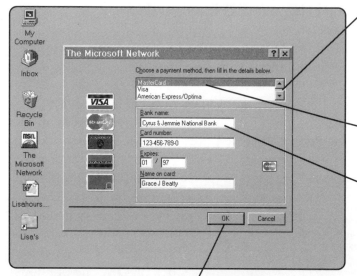

6. **Click** on the ▼ or ▲ to scroll through the credit card list until you see the type of card you'll be using to pay for your account.

7. **Click** on the **type of credit card** you will use.

8. **Type** the **information** called for and **press** the **Tab key**. The cursor will move to the next box.

9. **Continue** in this way until all the information is filled in.

10. **Click** on **OK**. The previous Microsoft Network dialog box will reappear.

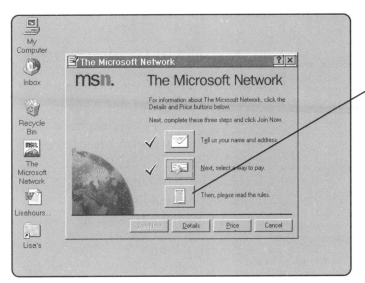

Reading the Rules

1. **Click** on the **icon** next to "Then, please read the rules." Another Microsoft Network dialog box will appear.

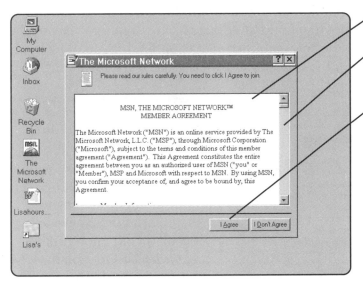

2. **Read** the **rules**.

3. **Scroll down** to see them all.

4. **Click** on **I Agree**. If you do not agree to the rules and click on I Don't Agree, the setup will end. You must agree to the rules to become a member.

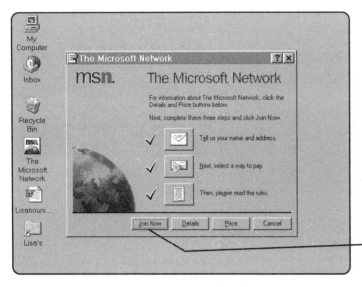

Selecting Phone Numbers

You connect to MSN through the phone lines. Now it's time to select the phone number(s) you want to use to dial in to MSN. You'll select local numbers from the updated list that was downloaded a few minutes ago.

1. Click on **Join Now**. Another Microsoft Network dialog box will appear.

The program will select phone numbers for you and enter them into these boxes. However, they may not be the best (least expensive) option for you. If no local numbers were found, a message will tell you this.

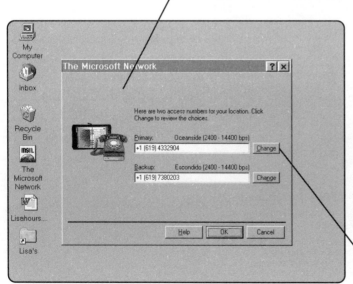

2. Get your **phone book**.

3. Look in the front for the pages that tell you which exchanges you can call without a toll under the terms of the service you are paying for. (You may also have to consult an old phone bill to see which service you have.) Toll charges can run up very quickly when you're online.

4. Click on **Change** for the Primary number. A list will appear.

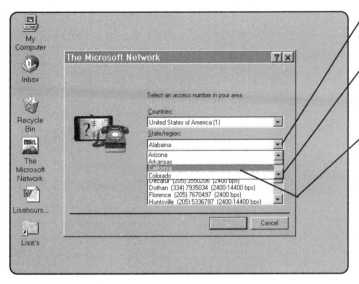

5. **Click** on the ▼ to open the list of states.

6. **Click repeatedly** on the ▼ until you see the name of the state you are calling from.

7. **Click** on the **name** of the state. Names of towns in the state will appear in the lower list box.

Next to each town name is a phone number. The first three digits (in parentheses) are the area code. The next three are the local exchange. If you live in a city, it's easy to find a toll-free local exchange. In the suburbs or the country, it may not be as easy.

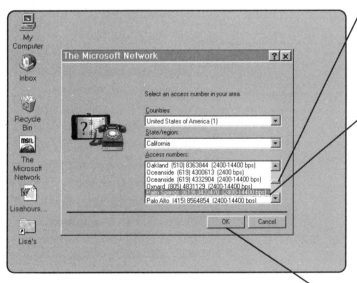

8. **Scroll** through the list, looking first for your area code, and second, for the local exchanges in your area code.

9. **Click** on a **town name** with a local exchange that you can call without toll charges. If none are available, select one that has the lowest toll charges possible. You may need to do a little calculating with your phone book in hand to find the least expensive number.

10. **Click** on **OK**.

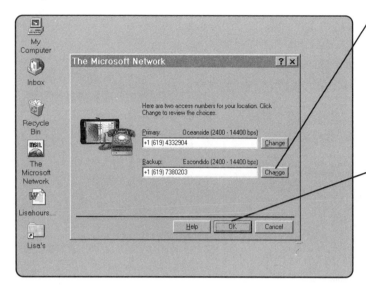

11. **Repeat steps 4–10** to select the Backup number. If there are not two toll-free local exchange numbers in your calling area, select the same number for both "Primary" and "Backup."

12. **Click** on **OK**. The numbers you selected will be stored by the program, and the Calling dialog box will appear.

SIGNING ON

You're finally ready to make contact with MSN. It'll be brief, but not as brief as when the list of local phone numbers was downloaded. This time you're sending off all the information that you entered into the forms a few pages back, and selecting a member ID and password.

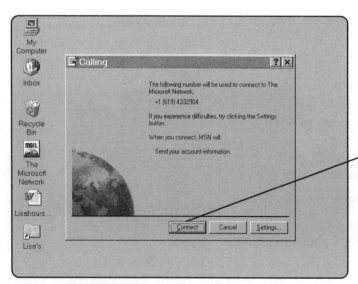

1. **Click** on **Connect**. After a few moments, you'll be connected to MSN, and another Microsoft Network dialog box will appear.

2. Type a **name** for yourself in the **Member ID** box. This is how you'll be known to others on the network, and it does not have to be your real name. You can be as creatively anonymous as you want, though you may want to keep the name short for convenience.

3. Click in the **Password** box to place the cursor.

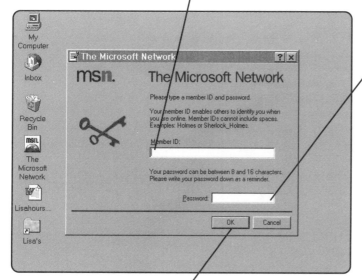

4. Type a **password**, between 8 and 16 characters long. Your password should be hard for others to guess. A made-up word that includes symbols, such as !@#$%, and numbers is best. Be sure to write your password down, and hide it in a place where you can find it if you forget it.

5. Click on **OK**. You will be disconnected, and another Microsoft Network dialog box will appear.

That's it! You're a member now, but there are still a few things to do.

6. Click on **Finish**. The dialog box will close.

OPENING EXCHANGE'S INBOX FOR THE FIRST TIME

Before you can use MSN's versatile electronic mail, you have to set up the Inbox. It's not complicated; a Wizard will walk you through it. If you have already opened the Inbox and done this, you can skip to the last page of this chapter.

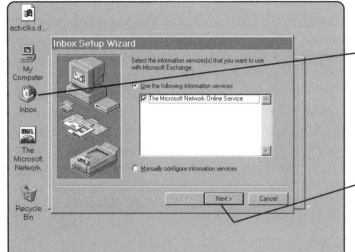

1. **Click twice** on the **Inbox icon**. The Inbox Setup Wizard dialog box that you see here will appear. "The Microsoft Network Online Service" will be selected.

2. **Click** on **Next**. Another Inbox Setup Wizard dialog box will appear.

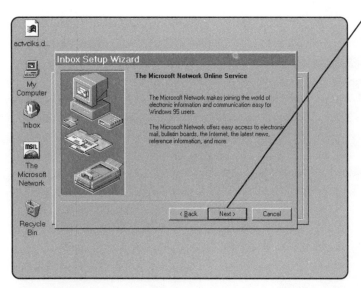

3. **Click** on **Next**. Another Inbox Setup Wizard dialog box will appear.

If you already have a personal address book on your computer, you'll know it. If this is the case, click on the Browse button and use standard Windows Explorer techniques to locate it for the Setup Wizard. If this is not the case, the Wizard will create an address book for you. You'll learn how to use it in Chapter 3.

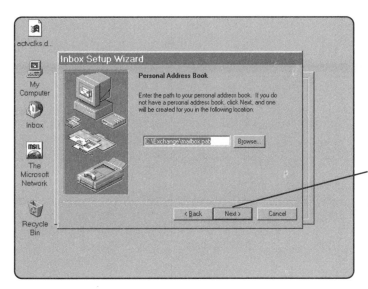

4. Click on **Next**. Another Inbox Setup Wizard dialog box will appear.

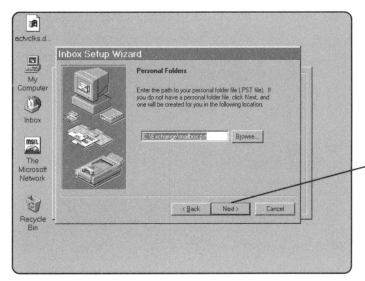

This dialog box has to do with where the folders for copies of your e-mail will be located on your hard disk. You'll learn about creating and using the folders in Chapter 4.

5. Click on **Next**. Another Inbox Setup Wizard dialog box will appear.

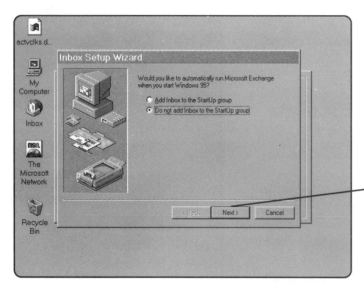

Notice that the second option, "Do not add Inbox to the StartUp group," already has a dot in the circle. We recommend that you stick with this option. You'll learn more about the Inbox in Chapters 3 and 4.

6. Click on **Next**. Another Inbox Setup Wizard dialog box will appear.

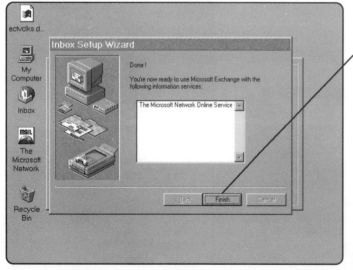

All done!

7. Click on **Finish**.

The Exchange screen will appear as the Inbox finishes setting itself up and opens for the first time. You'll also see this each time you use the Inbox. You'll explore the Inbox in Chapter 4. For now, just close it and we'll show you how to take care of one more detail.

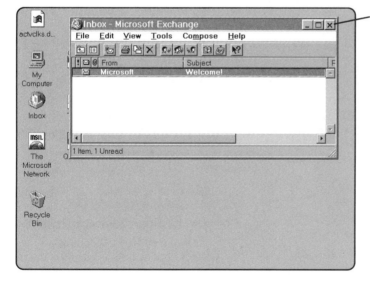

8. **Click** on the **Close box** ([×]) in the Inbox – Microsoft Exchange title bar. The Inbox will close.

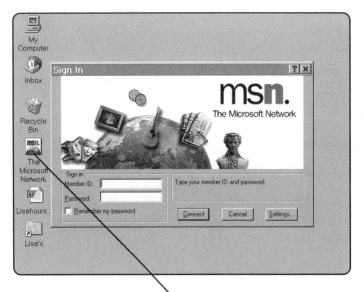

STORING YOUR NAME AND PASSWORD

The Sign In dialog box can store your name and password to make connecting easier for you. Anyone who can use your computer will be able to sign on to your account if you do this. You have to sign on to do it, so if you don't want to connect at this time, just remember to take these steps the next time you do.

1. Click twice on **The Microsoft Network icon**. The Sign In box will appear.

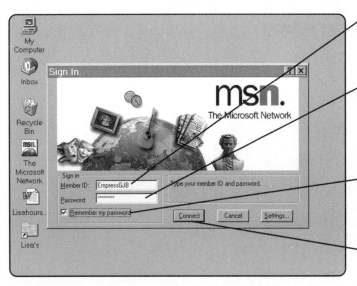

2. Type your **Member ID** in the Member ID box and press the Tab key.

3. Type your **password** in the Password box. Notice that stars are substituted for the characters.

4. Click on **"Remember my password"** to place a ✔ in the box.

5. Click on **Connect**. You'll be connected to the network.

The first time you connect, you will be asked to fill out a Member Personal Profile (not shown here). You will also receive a welcome message from Bill Gates.

Connecting to MSN

There are several ways to make using MSN easier and to give your screen a look you like. We'll show you these in this chapter, and also give you a quick look at the network so that you will know your way around a little better. In this chapter, you will do the following:

✔ Sign on to MSN for the first time

✔ See where a few things on the network are located

✔ Fine-tune the MSN program to suit your tastes

SIGNING ON

1. **Click twice** on **The Microsoft Network icon**. The Sign In dialog box will appear.

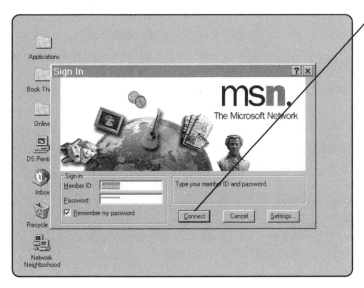

2. **Click** on **Connect.** After a few moments, The Microsoft Network MSN Central window and a welcome message may appear. A few moments after that, MSN Today will appear.

The first time you connect to MSN, you may get a greeting from Bill Gates and a member questionnaire. Finish filling out the questionnaire and send it to MSN. Click on the Close button (⨯) on the title bar of the welcome message after you read it.

Ordinarily when you sign on, first you will see the MSN Central window. It acts like a main menu with links to services in the network. Next, MSN Today will open, as shown below.

MSN Today changes daily to show you what's happening on the network. It works like a menu. You can click on an image, or on one of the things listed in white text along its left border, to get more information on the item. See Chapter 5 for more on MSN Today.

MSN looks and behaves the way it does because of how it has been set up by the Microsoft programmers. Many of its *default*, or standard settings can be changed. One of these default settings causes MSN Today to open automatically each time you sign on.

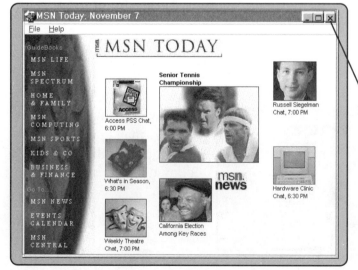

3. **Click** on the **Close button** (⨯). MSN Today will close.

SHOWING THE TOOLBAR

MSN includes a toolbar with several handy buttons.

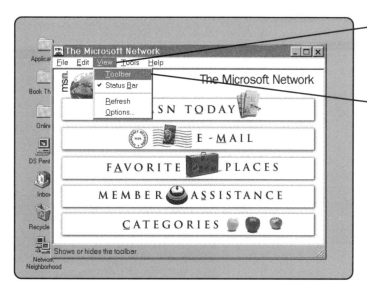

1. **Click** on **View** in the menu bar. The View menu will appear.

2. **Click** on **Toolbar**. The menu will close and the toolbar will appear.

If you want to use the toolbar, you'll have to open it separately in every window that appears in MSN. Also, the next time you sign on, the toolbar may not be there.

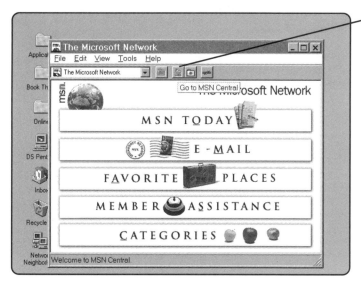

To see what a button does, rest the mouse pointer over it. A tag will appear after a moment. In the example shown here, "Go to MSN Central" appears. Since we're already at MSN Central, the button is grayed out, indicating that it can't be used here.

SETTING YOUR OPTIONS

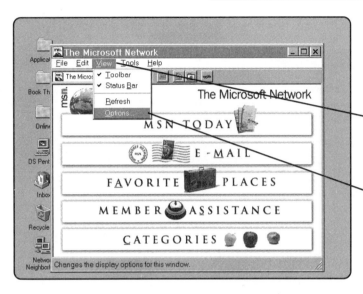

Now we'll show you where some of the default settings we mentioned earlier are located.

1. Click on **View** in the menu bar. The View menu will appear.

2. Click on **Options**. The Options dialog box will open with the General tab on top.

The General tab of the dialog box includes two settings that we'll deal with.

If you're connected to MSN and don't do anything for a while, it will automatically disconnect. The upper setting tells MSN how long to wait while you're not interacting with the network before disconnecting. You can click on the ▲ and ▼ buttons to change the number of minutes.

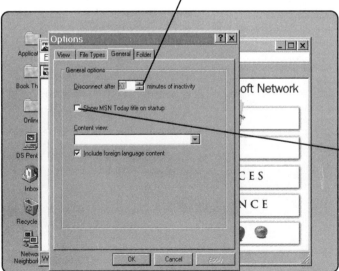

If you do not want MSN Today to open when you sign on, click here to remove the ✔ from the box.

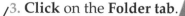

3. Click on the **Folder tab**.

You can either have a sep
each MSN folder you vi

windo
close it by acci
happens, you may ha
difficulty getting back or
worse, completely lose track
of the fact that you're online.
We recommend the separate
window option because
of this.

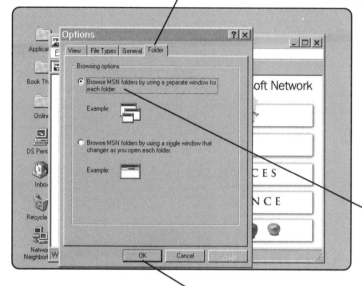

4. Click on **"Browse MSN folders by using a separate window …"** to place a dot in the circle.

5. Click on **OK** to save your options.

Changing Your Password

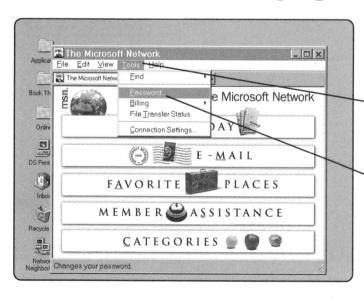

It's recommended that you change your password regularly for security.

1. Click on **Tools** in the menu bar. The Tools menu will appear.

2. Click on **Password**. The Change Your Password dialog box will appear.

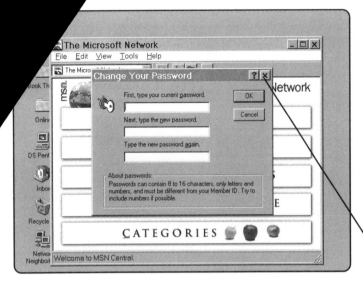

To change your password, you have to type the old one in the top box, then type the new one in the middle and lower boxes. You have to click the OK button to save the change. If you change your password, be sure to write the new one down and keep it where you won't lose it.

3. **Click** on the **Close button** ([X]). The dialog box will close.

EXPLORING MSN

❖ MSN TODAY is shown earlier in this chapter, and in more detail in Chapter 5.

❖ E-MAIL opens Exchange. (See Chapters 3 and 4.)

❖ FAVORITE PLACES is where you can store shortcuts to places in MSN that you want to revisit often. Saving Favorite Places is demonstrated later in this chapter.

❖ MEMBER ASSISTANCE is where you go for answers to your questions about MSN.

1. **Click** on **CATEGORIES**. The Categories window will open.

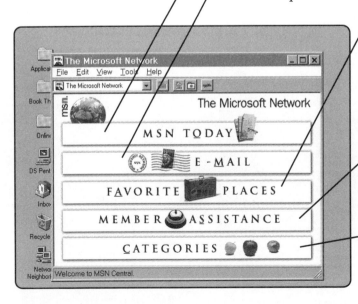

Changing the View

"Categories" is where things start to get interesting. Each category contains folders for different general subject areas. Each subject area folder will open to show more detailed folders. The detailed folders contain *bulletin boards* (where members can exchange messages), links to Internet newsgroups, World Wide Web sites, and more.

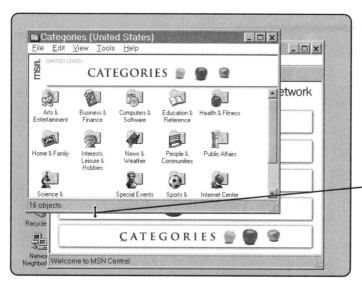

1. **Move** your **mouse pointer** to the lower edge of the window. As you do, it will turn into a two-headed arrow pointing up and down.

2. **Press** and **hold** the **mouse button** and **drag** the lower edge of the window down. The window will become larger, making it easier to see all of the icons.

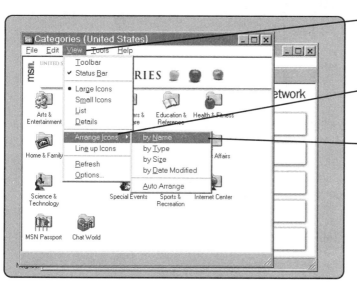

3. **Click** on **View** in the menu bar. The View menu will appear.

4. **Click** on **Arrange Icons**. Another menu will appear.

5. **Click** on **by Name**. The icons will be rearranged and appear in alphabetical order by name.

You can also change from icons to a detailed list that shows what each object, or item, in the window is.

6. Click on **View** in the menu bar. The View menu will appear.

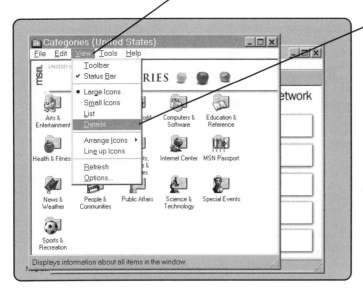

7. Click on **Details**. The icons will change to a detailed list.

8. Repeat Step 6 to open the View menu.

9. Click on **Toolbar**. The toolbar will appear.

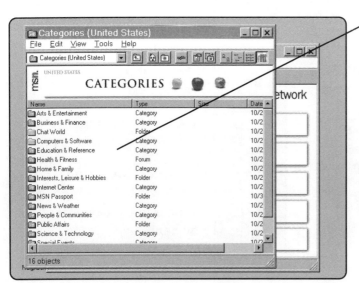

This list shows each object's name, what it is, and when it was created. It is like the detailed list you can have in My Computer or Windows Explorer.

10. Repeat steps 6 and 7, but select Large Icons instead of Details. The detailed list will change back to icons.

Moving Around

The toolbar provides a tree list that shows where you are in MSN. You can use it to move between the branches.

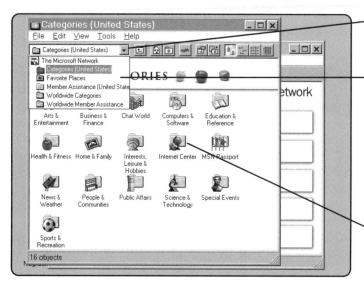

1. Click on the ▼ in the list box. A list will appear.

You can click on anything in this list to go to it. If you open one of the selections in the Categories folder here, its name will appear indented under Categories (United States) in the list.

2. Click twice on **Internet Center**. The Internet Center window will appear.

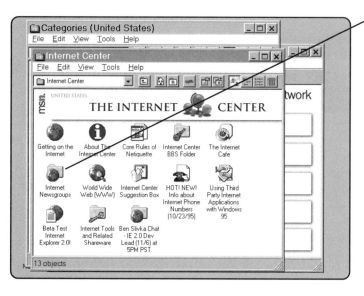

3. Click twice on **Internet Newsgroups**. The Internet Newsgroups window will appear.

GETTING FULL ACCESS TO INTERNET NEWSGROUPS

The great majority of Internet newsgroups deal with topics of general interest. However, there are a few that are of an adult nature. The default MSN setting will not allow access to all Internet newsgroups because of this. You have to send MSN an electronic form stating that you are an adult and that you want access to all of the newsgroups to use them. The "eform," as it is called, is in a separate folder.

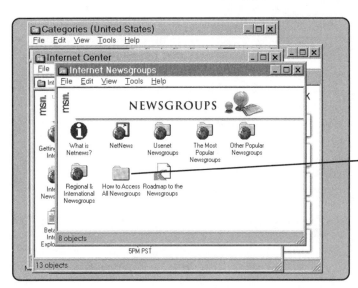

1. Click twice on **How to Access All Newsgroups**. The How to Access All Newsgroups window will appear.

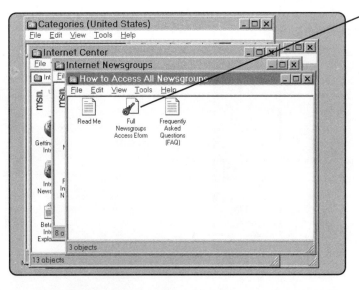

2. Click twice on the **Full Newsgroups Access Eform icon**. A Downloading window will appear.

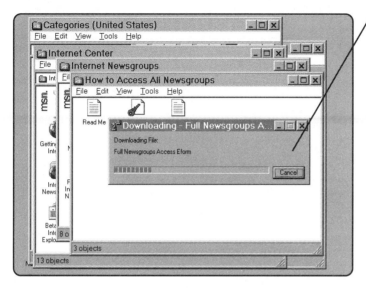

The Downloading message window tracks the progress of a download. "Download" means to receive a file from another computer. When it is finished, the Full Access EForm window will appear.

If you are over 18 and want access to all newsgroups, check the box and send in the form. You can also remove access once it has been established, by clicking on the Remove Access tab and sending in the form that will appear.

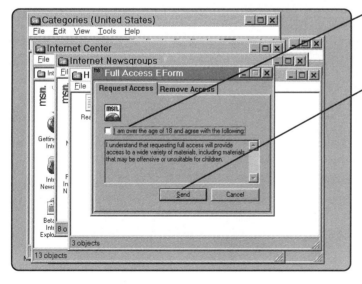

3. **Click** on **"I am over the age of 18…"** to place a ✔ in the box.

4. **Click** on **Send**. The form will be sent to MSN, and the dialog box will disappear.

5. **Click** on the **Close button** (⊠) of the How to Access All Newsgroups window to close it.

ADDING FAVORITE PLACES

If you want to be able to get back to this (or any) folder quickly, just add it to your Favorite Places. As you may recall, Favorite Places is one of the options on the MSN Central screen that you see when you first sign on.

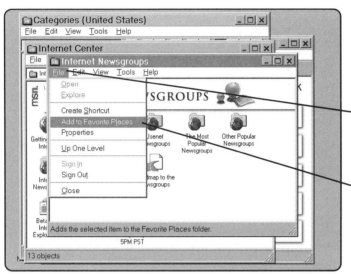

1. **Click** on **File** in the menu bar. The File menu will appear.

2. **Click** on **Add to Favorite Places**. The next time you check Favorite Places, an icon for the folder will be there.

SAYING GOOD-BYE

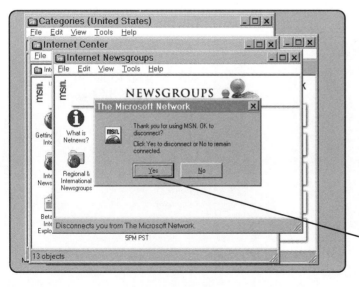

Now you're ready to move on and learn about MSN in more detail. But first, we'll show you how to disconnect from the service.

1. **Repeat Step 1**, above, to open the File menu.

2. **Click** on **Sign Out**. A dialog box will appear.

3. **Click** on **Yes**. You will be disconnected from MSN.

The Microsoft Network

Part II: Using E-Mail

Customizing
Your Inbox

With Microsoft Exchange and The Microsoft Network, you have an electronic post office at your fingertips. Microsoft Exchange is a program that not only provides e-mail service, but also has an address book and a filing system to help you keep your correspondence organized. You can compose your mail, edit your address book, and sort your mail without even being connected to MSN. In this chapter, you will do the following:

✔ Add sound to Microsoft Exchange

✔ Choose a Spelling option

✔ Set up an Address Book

✔ Customize a toolbar

✔ Create a new folder

OPENING
MICROSOFT EXCHANGE

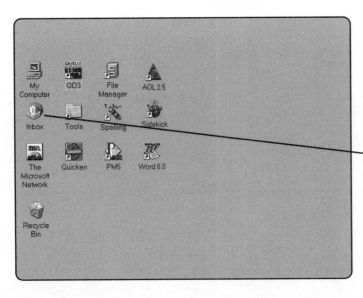

To open Microsoft Exchange, you use the Inbox icon located on your Windows 95 desktop. The desktop shown here has been customized; yours will look different.

1. **Click twice** on the **Inbox icon** to open the program. After a long intermission, the Inbox – Microsoft Exchange window will appear.

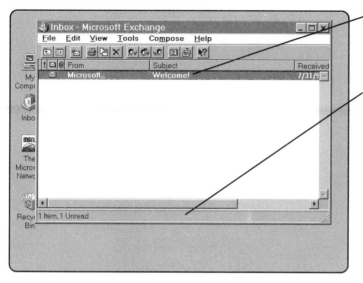

Notice that a Welcome letter from Microsoft is waiting for you.

The status of the letter "1 item, 1 unread" appears in the status bar at the bottom of the window. (In Chapter 4 you will take the time to read the letter and move it to a new folder.)

CHANGING THE VIEW

If your screen looks like the screen above, complete the following step to make it look like the screen shown below.

1. **Click** on the **Show/Hide Folder List icon** on the toolbar. It's the second icon from the left. A list of folders will appear.

Notice that the Inbox folder is open and that Inbox is in bold type indicating that there is unread mail. The Inbox folder is where your Welcome letter is located.

MAKING YOUR MAILBOX LOOK AND SOUND THE WAY YOU WANT IT TO

If you have a sound card, you can make your mailbox beep when you get mail. In addition to sound, there are numerous other options you can set.

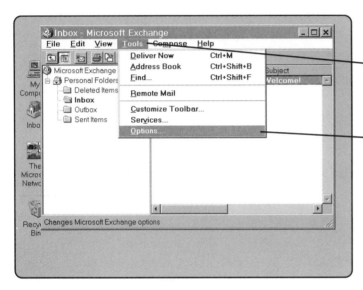

1. Click on **Tools** in the menu bar. The Tools menu will appear.

2. Click on **Options**. The Options dialog box will appear with the General tab on top.

Notice the settings that have been preset and already have a ✔ in their box. These are called *default* settings and can be changed. If your computer has a sound card, "Play a sound" will be checked.

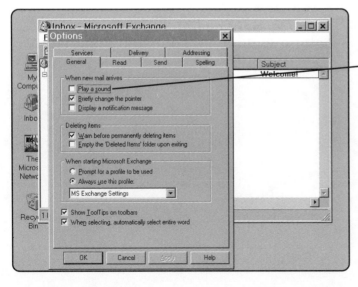

3. Click on **"Play a sound"** to remove the ✔ from the box if you do not want Exchange to make a sound when mail is received. (Your computer must have a sound card installed to use this option.)

4. Click on **any box** with a ✔ in it if you want to add or remove any other options.

Choosing Spelling Options

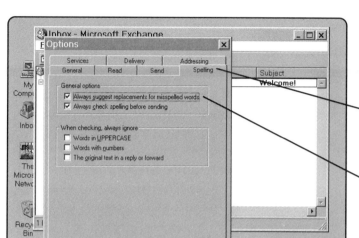

If you have Microsoft Office or Word 7 installed on your machine, you will be able to use the spell check feature.

1. Click on the **Spelling tab** to bring it to the front of the dialog box.

2. Click on a **box** to place a ✔ in it to choose a particular option. In this example, we chose "Always suggest replacements for misspelled words" and "Always check spelling before sending."

3. Click on **OK**. The Inbox – Microsoft window will appear.

Before you begin to set up your address book, take a moment to go through this next section on Internet addresses.

DEALING WITH INTERNET ADDRESSES

The first rule of sending e-mail is to have the person you're writing to give you his or her address. There is not an easy way to look up someone's Internet address because there isn't a comprehensive directory of people who can receive e-mail on the Internet. Internet addresses can be confusing at first glance, but they do follow a specific format. Let's take a closer look at the parts of an Internet address.

The first part of an Internet address is a person's name, e.g., bbunny or efudd.

The person's name is always followed by @, for "at."

Examples of Internet Addresses

bbunny@acs.bu.edu
efudd@crsa.bu.edu

The part of the address after the @ depends on how complicated the address is. For example, if you live in an apartment building, your address has more parts to it than if you live in a single house. You have to give your apartment number as well as your street address. The same is true of an Internet address.

It helps to look at the last element in the address first. The last element in these addresses is "edu." This is one of the six major categories that describe the types of Internet accounts. The six categories or *domains*, are listed in the box below. The "edu" domain name tells you that these are educational accounts.

The next part of the address (bu) tells you that this is a Boston University account.

The two Boston University addresses have different letters after @ because Boston University has many different computers hooked to the Internet.

Each of these parts of the address is followed by a period (.), called a "dot" in online talk, or *dotspeak*. The dot separates the parts of the address. If you want to sound like one of the "in crowd," read the first name above as "bbunny at acs dot bu dot edu."

Internet Categories

com = commercial
edu = educational
gov = government
mil = military
net = networks
org = organizations

You may also see 2-letter country codes, such as us for the United States, cn for Canada, and jp for Japan.

Making an Online Address into an Internet Address

As a member of The Microsoft Network, you have to add elements to your MSN address to make it an Internet address. This is true of addresses in all of the online services. For most online services, there is one simple formula:

Making an Online Service Address Into an Internet Address

❶ ❷ ❸ ❹❺
| | | | |
123456@mcimail.com (an MCI Mail address)

gbgroup@msn.com (an MSN address)

write.bks@aol.com (an America Online address)

12345.678@compuserve.com (a CompuServe address)

❶ **Type** the person's **screen name** or identification number (also called a user ID).

❷ **Type @** after the individual's name.

❸ **Type** the **name** of the online service.

❹ **Type** a **dot**.

❺ **Type com** to identify it as a commercial service.

There are some things you should know about these Internet addresses:

❖ It doesn't matter whether you type the name in all uppercase letters, all lowercase letters, or a combination. Addresses are not case sensitive. GBGROUP is the same as GBGroup and gbgroup.

❖ A CompuServe user ID number has a comma (12345,678). The Internet doesn't recognize commas in e-mail addresses, so the comma must be changed to a dot (i.e., 12345.678).

SETTING UP THE ADDRESS BOOK

It's easier to address an e-mail letter when you have the person to whom the letter will be sent listed in the address book.

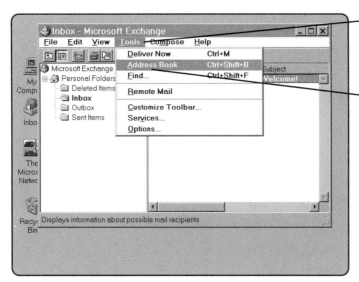

1. **Click** on **Tools** in the menu bar. The Tools menu will appear.

2. **Click** on **Address Book**. The Address Book window will appear.

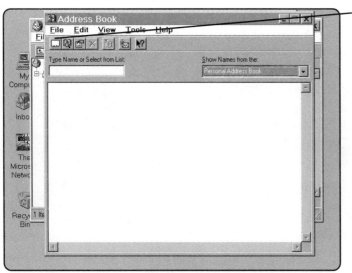

3. **Click** on the **New Entry button** in the toolbar. The New Entry dialog box will appear.

Adding an Internet Address

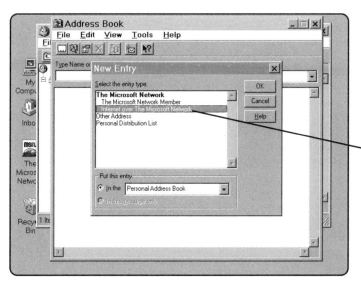

In this example, the person we will be adding to the address book does not have a Microsoft Network account. Therefore, the letter will be sent via the Internet.

1. **Click** on **Internet over The Microsoft Network**.

2. **Click** on **OK**. The New Internet over The Microsoft Network Properties dialog box will appear.

3. **Type** the recipient's **screen name or ID number** and **press** the **Tab key**.

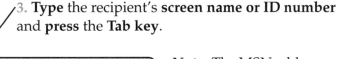

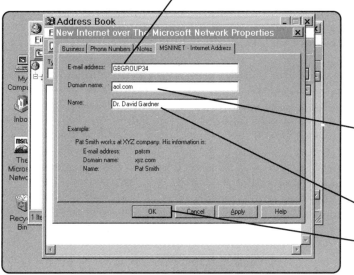

Note: The MSN address book will automatically add the @ to the Internet address for you, so don't include it here.

4. **Type** the **domain name** and **press** the **Tab key**. In this example, it is aol.com.

5. **Type** the **person's name**.

6. **Click** on **OK**. The dialog box will close.

Adding a Microsoft Network Address

In this example, you will add a Microsoft Network member's address to the Address Book.

1. **Follow steps 1–2** in the section, "Setting up the Address Book," if needed, to open the Address Book dialog box.

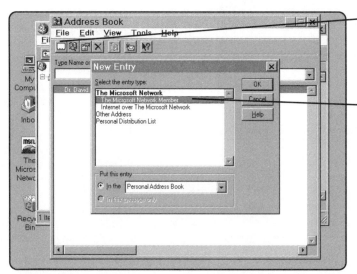

2. **Click** on the **New Entry button** in the toolbar. The New Entry dialog box will appear.

3. **Click** on **The Microsoft Network Member**.

4. **Click** on **OK**. The New The Microsoft Network Member Properties dialog box will appear.

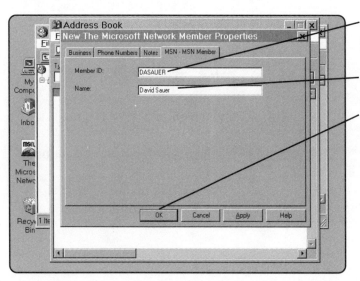

5. **Type** the **member's ID** and **press** the **Tab key**.

6. **Type** the **member's name**.

7. **Click** on **OK**. The dialog box will close.

EDITING AN ADDRESS

In this example, you will correct an e-mail address.

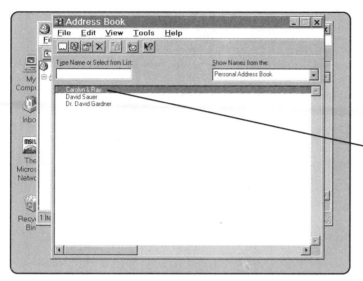

1. Click twice on the **name** of the person whose address you want to edit. In this example, it is Carolyn & Ray. The Carolyn & Ray Properties dialog box will appear.

Notice that the text in the E-mail address text box is highlighted.

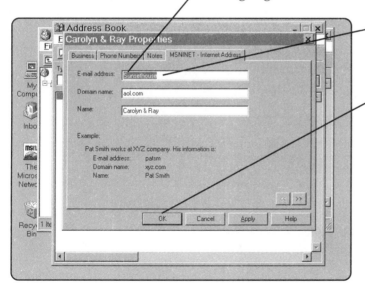

2. Type the correct **e-mail address**. It will replace the highlighted text.

3. Click on **OK**. The dialog box will close.

DELETING A NAME FROM THE ADDRESS BOOK

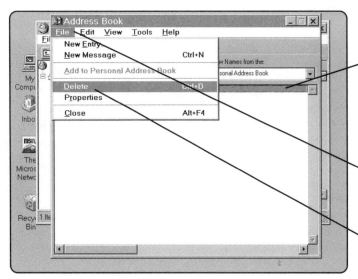

It's also easy to delete entries from the address book.

1. Click on the **name** that you want to delete from the Address Book to highlight it. (In this example the name is covered by the File menu.)

2. Click on **File** in the menu bar. The File menu will appear.

3. Click on **Delete**. A Microsoft Exchange dialog box will appear.

4. Click on **Yes**. The name and address will be deleted from the Address Book, and the dialog box will disappear.

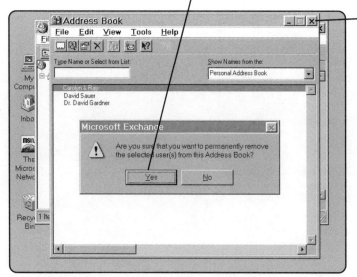

5. Click on the **Close button** ([X]) on the Address Book window. The Inbox – Microsoft Exchange window will reappear.

CUSTOMIZING A TOOLBAR

The toolbars in Microsoft Exchange can be customized. In this example, you will add the Deliver Now button to the main toolbar. Other toolbars can be customized in the same way.

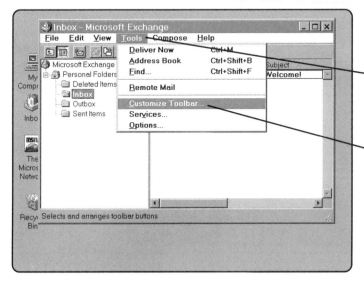

1. **Click** on **Tools** in the menu bar. The Tools menu will appear.

2. **Click** on **Customize Toolbar**. The Customize Toolbar dialog box will appear.

3. **Click** on the lower part of the **scroll bar** to scroll down the list of available buttons.

4. **Click** on **Tools – Deliver Now** to highlight it.

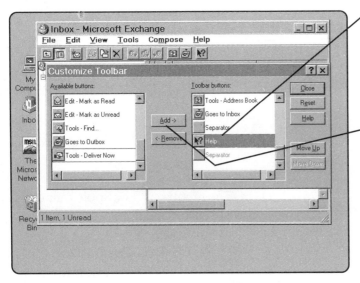

5. **Click** on the **Help button**. The Deliver Now button will appear to the left of the Help button when it is added to the toolbar.

6. **Click** on **Add**.

7. **Click** on **Close**. Deliver Now will be added to the toolbar.

REMOVING A BUTTON FROM THE TOOLBAR

1. **Follow steps 1–2** in "Customizing a Toolbar" to open the Customize Toolbar dialog box.

2. **Click** on the **button** that you want to remove from the toolbar to highlight it.

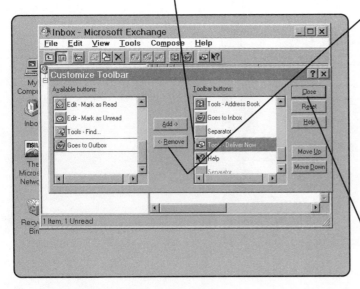

3. **Click** on **Remove**. The button will be removed from the toolbar and added to the Available buttons list. In this example, we did not actually remove the Deliver Now button.

Note: To restore a toolbar to its original setup, click on the Reset button.

4. **Click** on **Close**. The Microsoft Network window will appear.

46

ADDING A FOLDE

Microsoft has already started to organi~
personal filing cabinet for you with the folu~
here. It's very easy to ada
other folders to suit your
own way of organizing
things. For this example,
you'll add a folder for
received mail.

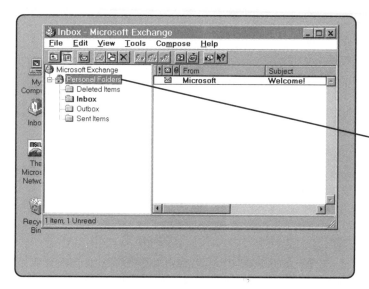

1. Click on **Personal Folders**
to highlight it.

2. Click on **File** in the menu bar. The File menu
will appear.

3. Click on **New Folder**.
The New Folder dialog box
will appear.

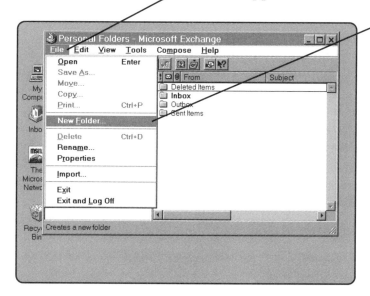

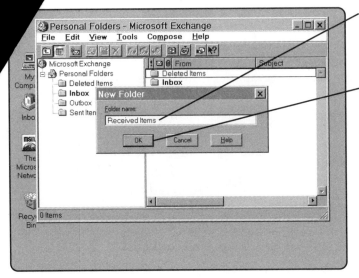

4. Type the **name** for the new folder. In this example we'll call it Received Items.

5. Click on **OK**.

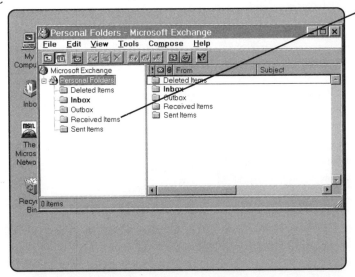

Notice that the folder has been added to your list of Personal Folders. In the next chapter you will move mail to this folder.

Using Exchange for MSN E-mail

You can use The Microsoft Network's mail service to send electronic mail to anyone in the world whose computer is on The Microsoft Network, or who is connected to the Internet in some way. Because charges add up quickly we recommend that you go to Inbox and compose your mail offline (before you sign on to MSN). Then, after you have signed on to MSN, your outgoing mail will be delivered and incoming letters will be posted to your Inbox. In this chapter, you will do the following:

✔ Read new mail

✔ Move a file to a new folder

✔ Compose, send, and deliver mail

✔ Attach a file to a letter

✔ Respond to new mail

READING THE WELCOME LETTER

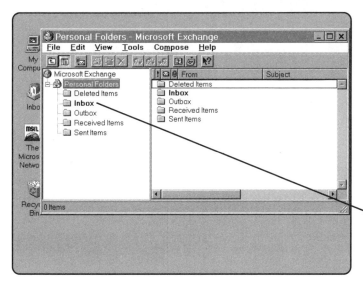

In this section, you will read the Welcome letter, if you haven't already peeked at it. The Welcome letter will automatically be waiting for you the first time you open the Inbox.

1. **Open** the **Inbox**, if you haven't already done so.

2. **Click** on the **Inbox folder** to open it. This is the folder where new mail is stored.

Notice that both the Inbox folder and the Welcome letter titles are in boldface. The bold type indicates that mail waiting in the Inbox has not been read.

Notice also that the status of items in the folder appears in the status bar at the bottom of the window.

3. **Click twice** on **Welcome** to open the letter.

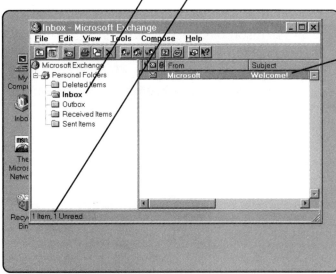

Printing the Welcome Letter

Computers are great, but it is sometimes easier and faster to read mail from a printed copy.

1. **Click** on the **Print button** in the toolbar. A Printing dialog box will appear.

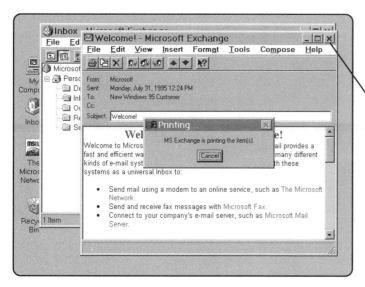

After a moment, the dialog box will disappear, and your letter will print.

2. Click on the **Close button** (🗙) to return to the Inbox – Microsoft Exchange window.

MOVING A FILE

In this section, you will move, or "drag-and-drop," the Welcome letter to a different folder for storage. See Chapter 3 for directions on creating a new folder.

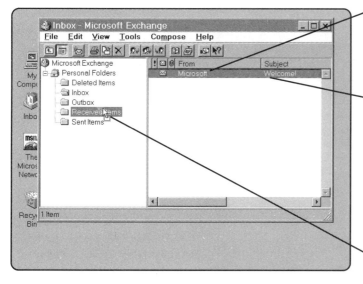

1. Click on **Welcome** to highlight it. Notice that the boldface type is gone because the letter has been read.

2. Place the **mouse pointer** over the highlighted text.

3. Press and hold the **mouse button** as you **drag** the pointer to the folder. The pointer will appear to have a little letter attached to it.

4. Release the **mouse button** when the folder becomes highlighted. The letter will now be in the other folder.

COMPOSING E-MAIL

In this section, you will write a letter to a member of The Microsoft Network and send a copy of the letter to another member. To save your connect time and money, remember to do this before you sign on to the network.

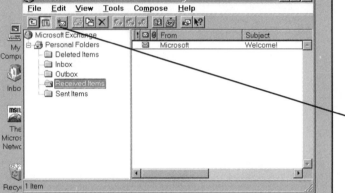

Addressing E-mail

1. Click on the **New Message button** in the toolbar. The New Message window will appear.

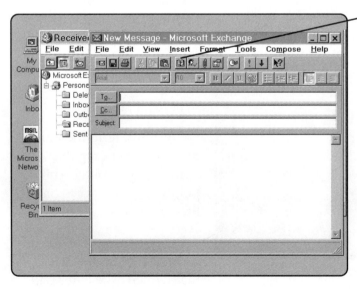

2. Click on the **Address Book button** in the toolbar. The Address Book dialog box will appear.

Note: One idiosyncrasy of the Inbox is that when you address e-mail offline, as you are doing in this example, you must use the address book. When you address e-mail while you are online, you can type an address directly into the To box, even if the address isn't in the address book.

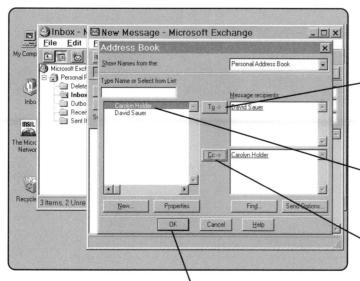

3. **Click** on the **name** of the person to whom the letter will be sent to highlight it.

4. **Click** on the **To button**. The name will appear in the Message recipients box and will be underlined.

5. **Click** on the **name** of the person to whom a copy of the letter will be sent.

6. **Click** on the **Cc button**. The name will appear in the Message recipients box and will be underlined.

7. **Click** on **OK**. The Microsoft Exchange dialog box will appear.

Writing the Letter

Microsoft Exchange has many features that you'd find in a word processing program. You can change the font or type style. You can stylize your e-mail with color, bulleted lists, centered text, italics, underlining, and other formatting features.

Note: These special effects will appear only on the e-mail of people who are also on The Microsoft Network, or who have an e-mail program that supports RTF, which stands for *rich text formatting*. If you are sending your e-mail through the Internet, your formatting will most likely be lost. The recipient of your letter will get only the text and won't see any of the special touches you've added.

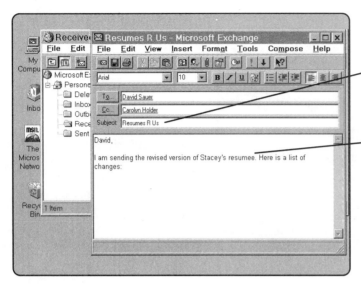

1. **Press** the **Tab key twice** to go the Subject box.

2. **Type** a **title** for your letter in the Subject box and **press** the **Tab key**.

3. **Type** the **body** of your text as shown here. We purposely misspelled "resumee," so that we could show you how to use spell checker later in this chapter.

Using Bullets

Bullets are a great tool to use in a letter when you are making a list. The Bullets button works like a toggle switch, and you can easily turn it on or off.

1. When you are ready to insert a bullet into your letter, **press** the **Enter key** to move to a new line.

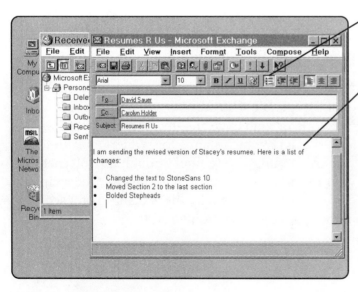

2. **Click** on the **Bullets button** in the toolbar. A bullet will appear.

3. **Type** the **text**. Every time you press the Enter key you will move to a new line and another bullet will be inserted.

4. When you want to turn off the bullet function in your letter, **press** the **Enter key** to go to a new line. Another bullet will appear.

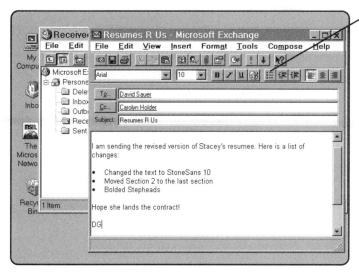

5. Click on the **Bullets button** in the toolbar. The bullet function will be turned off, and the bullet will disappear from the current line.

6. Finish typing the letter.

Changing a Font

In this section, you will change the font in the bulleted section of the letter.

1. Place the **cursor** in front of the text that you want to change.

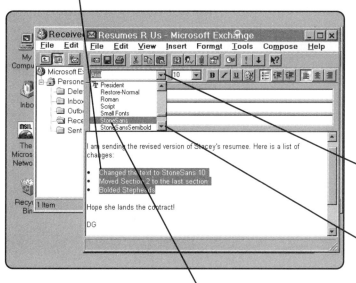

2. Press and hold the **mouse button** as you **drag** the cursor over the text.

3. Release the **mouse button** when the text you want to change is highlighted.

4. Click on the ▼ in the Font box. A drop-down list of fonts will appear.

5. Click on the ▼ to scroll down the list.

6. Click on the **font** of your choice. The list will close.

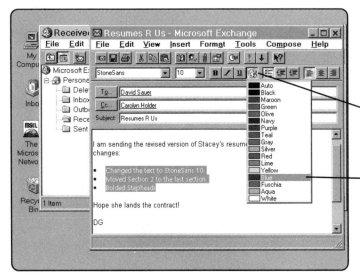

Adding Color

In this section, you will add color to the same text.

1. **Click** on the **Color button** in the toolbar. A drop-down list will appear.

2. **Click** on the **color** of your choice. The list will close.

3. **Click anywhere** on the letter to remove the highlighting.

CHECKING YOUR SPELLING

In this section, you will check the spelling in your letter.

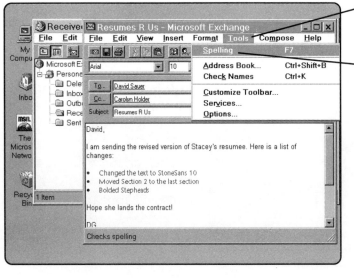

1. **Click** on **Tools**. The Tools menu will appear.

2. **Click** on **Spelling**. The Spelling dialog box will appear.

Correcting a Misspelled Word

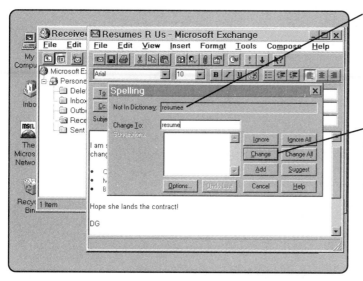

Notice that the first misspelled word appears in the Not in Dictionary box, and the corrected version appears in the Change To box.

1. Click on **Change** to replace the misspelled word. In this example, another Spelling dialog box will appear.

Adding a Word to the Dictionary

You can customize your dictionary by adding words to it. This means that the spelling checker will recognize the word in the future and won't tag it as a misspelled or unrecognized word.

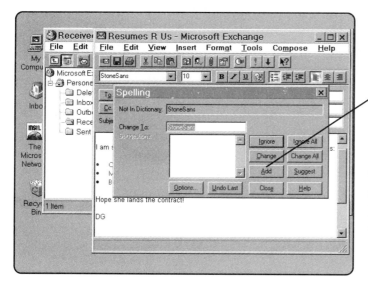

1. Click on **Add**. You will see an hourglass as the word is added to the dictionary.

Once the spelling check is finished, a Microsoft Exchange dialog box will appear.

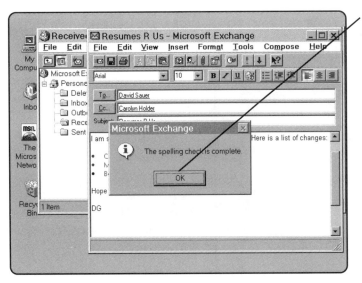

2. **Click** on **OK**. The letter window will reappear.

ATTACHING A FILE TO A LETTER

You can attach a file to your e-mail and send it to other members of Microsoft Exchange. You may not be able to send attached files to people on other online services, or over the Internet. Use regular

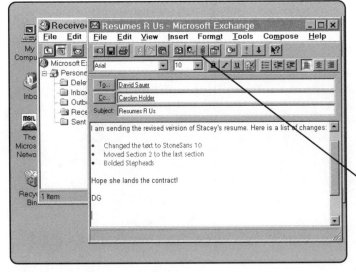

e-mail to check with the person you're sending the file to, to see if their e-mail system supports attached files. In this example, you will use standard Windows Explorer techniques to locate and attach a Word file to your letter.

1. **Click** on the **Insert File button** in the toolbar. (It has a picture of a paper clip on it.) The Insert File dialog box will appear.

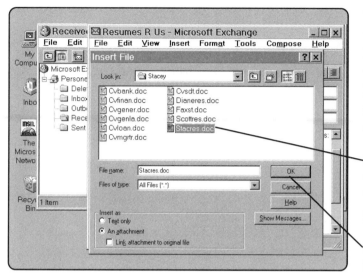

The Insert File dialog box works just like Windows Explorer. If you need help using Explorer techniques to locate the file you want to attach, consult Windows 95 online help.

2. **Click** on the **file** that you want to attach to your letter. The file name will appear in the File name text box.

3. **Click** on **OK**. The Insert File dialog box will close.

Notice that the file icon now appears on your document. This means that the file has been attached to your e-mail.

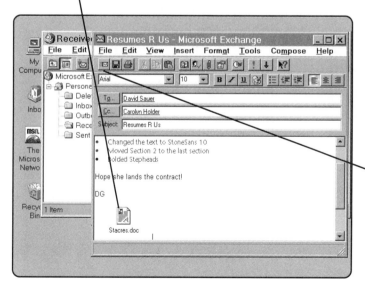

SENDING THE LETTER

When you have completed your letter, you will send the e-mail to your Outbox.

1. **Click** on the **Send button** in the toolbar. The letter window will close.

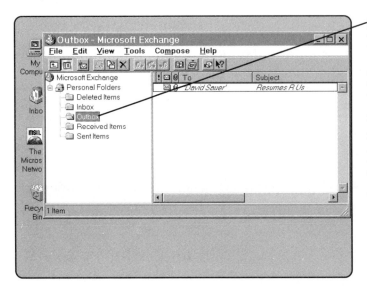

2. Click on the **Outbox Folder**. The folder will open.

Notice that the e-mail letter with the attachment has moved to the Outbox and is ready for delivery. The little paper clip next to the envelope means that there is a file attached.

DELIVERING E-MAIL

So far you have addressed and composed your letter offline. Now you will use a technique to sign on, deliver the letter, and then disconnect from the service. If there were e-mail waiting for you, it would be delivered to your computer, too. This method saves money by using the least possible amount of online time for e-mail.

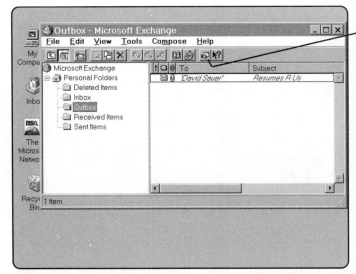

1. Click on the **Deliver Now button** in the toolbar. A Checking for New Messages dialog box will appear for a moment, then the Sign In dialog box will appear.

Note: If you did not add the Deliver Now button to the toolbar, as shown in Chapter 3, click on Tools in the menu bar, then click on Deliver Now.

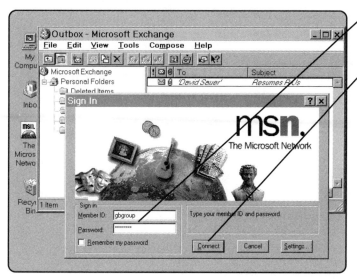

2. Type in your **name and password**, if necessary.

3. Click on **Connect**. After a few seconds, another New Messages dialog box will appear.

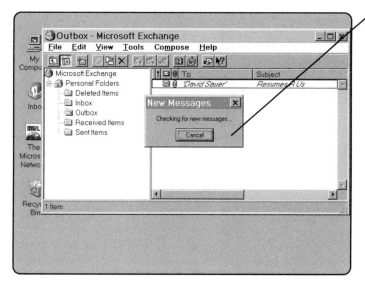

Don't panic if this dialog box lingers for a few seconds. This still beats going to the post office!

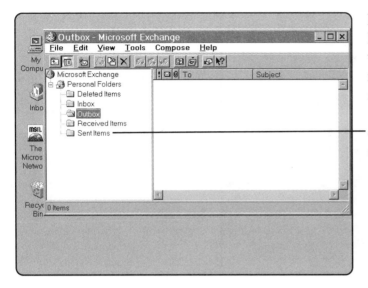

Notice that the letter has left the Outbox and, as you will see in the next step, has moved to the Sent Items folder.

4. **Click** on **Sent Items** to open the folder.

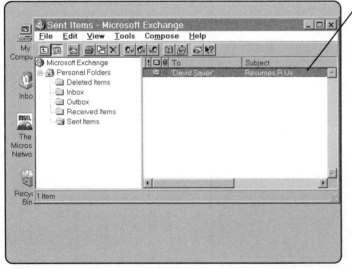

Voilà! Your e-mail has been sent.

As you can see, this process uses much less online time than signing on to the service, then composing your e-mail. If you're continuing on to the next section, you can skip the first two steps, since you've just done them.

RECEIVING MAIL

E-mail is held for you on the MSN computer, and you must go online to retrieve it.

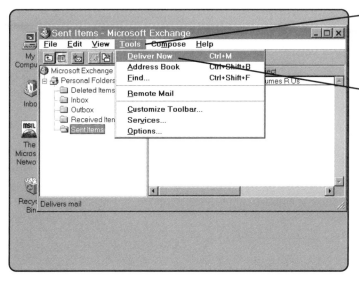

1. Click on **Tools** in the menu bar. The Tools menu will appear.

2. Click on **Deliver Now**. A Checking for New Messages box will appear briefly, then the Sign In dialog box will appear.

3. Follow steps 2–3 in the section, "Sending E-mail," to have the mail delivered to your Inbox.

Reading and Replying to E-mail

You can click twice on a letter in your Inbox to open the letter's window and read it, as we did with the Welcome letter at the beginning of this chapter. To reply, you click on the reply button in the letter's window, or do the following from the Inbox:

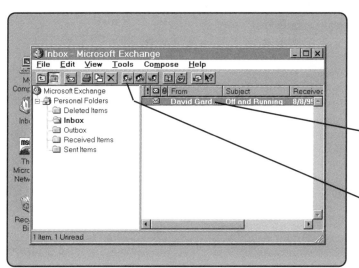

1. Click on the **letter that you want to reply to**. The letter will be highlighted.

2. Click on the **Reply to Sender button** in the toolbar. The RE: dialog box will appear.

The cursor will be blinking in a blank message area at the top of the original letter.

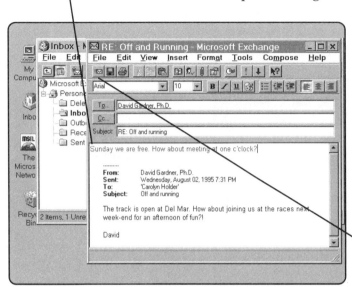

Note: If you do not want to include the original text in your reply, go to the Tools menu in the menu bar and click on Options. Next, click on the Read tab, and click on "Include the original text when replying" to remove the ✔ from the box.

3. **Type** your **response**.

4. **Click** on the **Send button** in the toolbar. The RE: dialog box will close.

5. **Click** on **Outbox**. The letter waiting to be delivered will appear in the Outbox list.

6. **Follow steps 1–4** in the section entitled "Delivering E-mail" to send your response.

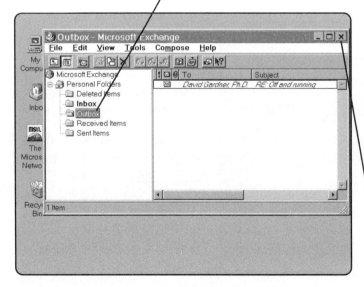

CLOSING MICROSOFT EXCHANGE

When you have finished "doing your mail" you can sign off in a flash.

1. **Click** on the **Close button** (⊠) in the title bar. Microsoft Exchange will close.

RECEIVING MAIL THROUGH THE MICROSOFT NETWORK

You can also receive mail automatically when you sign on to The Microsoft Network. In this example, we have the taskbar showing at the bottom of the screen so that you can see the status of the program as mail is being retrieved.

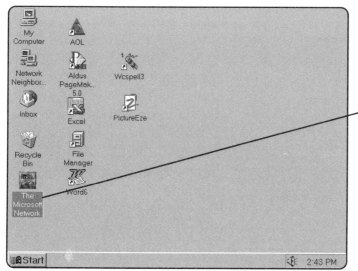

1. Click twice on **The Microsoft Network icon** on your desktop. The Sign In dialog box will appear.

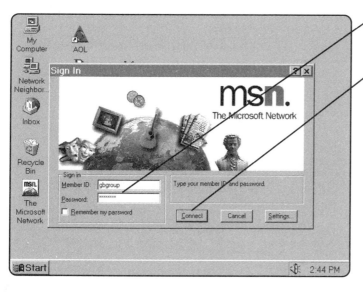

2. Type your **name and password**, if necessary.

3. Click on **Connect**. Once you're connected, if you have mail waiting to be delivered, a dialog box will appear saying that you have received new mail.

Notice that the modem icon is flashing in the status bar, and that the MSN icon is present, indicating that you are online. You may see only the message box, and not The Microsoft Network window shown behind it here.

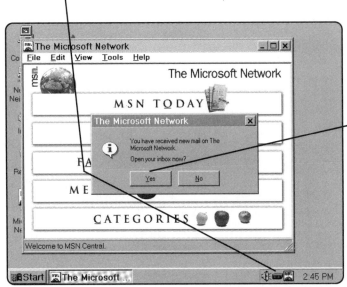

4. Click on **Yes**. The Microsoft Exchange program screen will appear. Then the Inbox – Microsoft Exchange window will appear. If your MSN setup is so configured (see Chapter 2), MSN Today may also appear in a few moments.

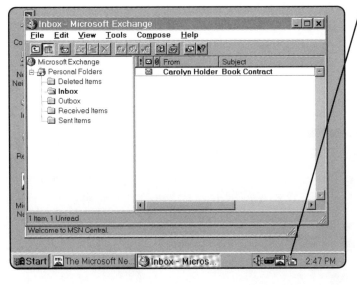

Notice that in this example there is a letter icon in the status bar, indicating that new mail has been received.

5. Click on the **Inbox folder** to open it, if it isn't open already. Your new mail will be listed.

DISCONNECTING FROM THE ONLINE SERVICE

Remember, because you signed on through The Microsoft Network program icon, you are still online. When you have finished using Microsoft Exchange, you need to close all open windows and disconnect from The Microsoft Network.

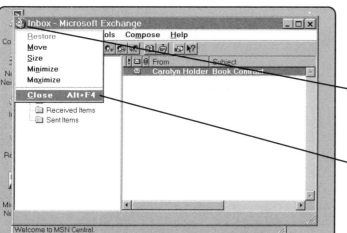

1. Click on the **Inbox icon** in the left corner of the Inbox title bar. A menu will appear.

2. Click on **Close**. Microsoft Exchange will close.

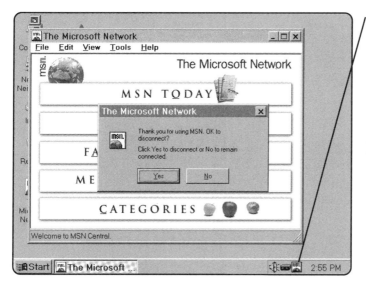

3. Click twice on the **MSN icon** on the right end of the taskbar. The Microsoft Network dialog box that you see here will appear.

4. Click on **Yes**. The Microsoft Network will close.

The Microsoft Network

Part III: Exploring MSN

Finding Out What's Happening on MSN

MSN Today and the Calendar of Events are The Microsoft Network's answer to the TV Guide. MSN Today will give you an overview of events that will be taking place on-line during the day. In the same manner, you can preview weekly coming attractions by reviewing the list of activities in the Calendar of Events. In this chapter, you will do the following:

✔ Check out today's events
✔ Review the key events for the upcoming week
✔ Review the daily schedule of events

EXPLORING MSN TODAY

In this section, you will preview today's online scheduled activities.

1. **Open The Microsoft Network** to **MSN Central**, if it isn't already on your screen.

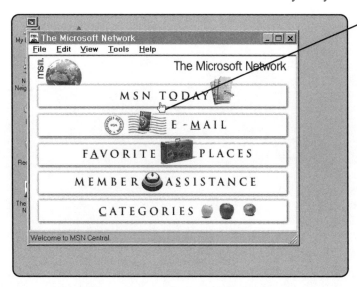

2. **Place** the **mouse arrow** on **MSN TODAY**. The arrow will turn into a hand. The mouse arrow will change to a hand each time you move the arrow over a link or shortcut.

3. **Click** on **MSN TODAY**. The Online Viewer window will appear briefly, then the MSN Today window will appear.

Notice that you will see a variety of pictures or icons that represent today's scheduled events. (Your screen will show different events than the ones shown here.)

4. Place the **mouse arrow** over the icon of an event that interests you. The arrow will turn into a hand.

5. Click on the **icon**. A pop-up window will appear with a brief description of the event and, if it is not ongoing, the time it will take place.

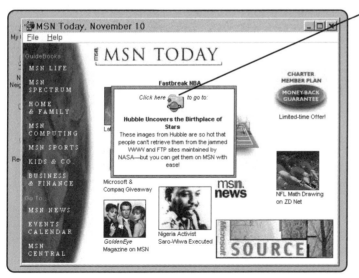

6. Click on the **icon**. Another dialog box or window will appear. In this example, it is the Astronomy & Space Forum.

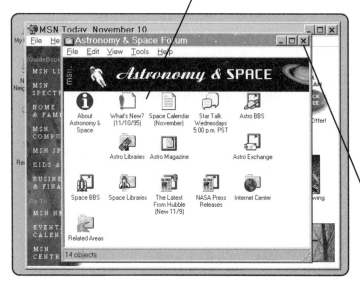

Notice another selection of icons and folders; in this example they are related to Astronomy & Space. By clicking on The Latest From Hubble, you will be able to locate and download NASA images from the Hubble Space Telescope. We'll demonstrate downloading files in another chapter, so we will return to MSN Today for now.

7. **Click** on the **Close Button** ([×]) in the Astronomy & Space Forum title bar to close the window.

REVIEWING THE CALENDAR OF EVENTS

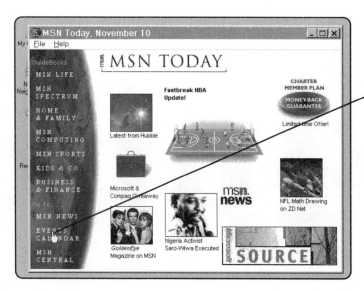

Now it is time to see what is on tap for the next week or so.

1. **Click** on **EVENTS CALENDAR**. The Online Viewer window will appear briefly, then the Calendar of Events window will appear.

The Calendar of Events window shows the key events happening within a two-week span. Let's take a more detailed look at a particular day.

2. Click on the **day** that contains the event you are interested in. The daily scheduled events window will appear.

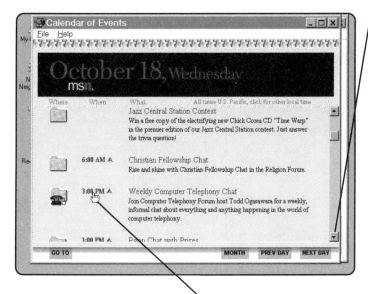

3. Click repeatedly on the ▼ to scroll through the list of events until you come to one that is scheduled for a particular time.

Verifying Time

Notice that the times posted here are PDT (Pacific Daylight Time). If you want to verify the time for a different time zone, click on the time next to the event you're interested in.

1. Click on the **time**. A pop-up window will appear.

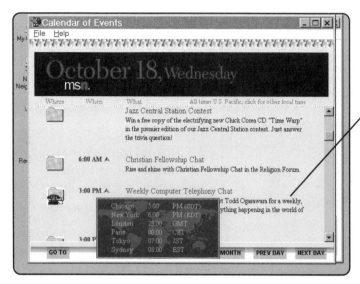

Notice that if you live in London, for example, the chat would take place at 23:00 GMT.

2. **Click anywhere** on the schedule to close the menu.

Checking Out the Location

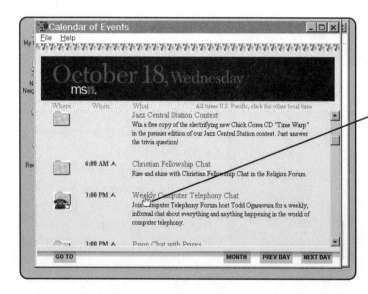

By selecting the colored text for an event, you can explore the event and the location that hosts it.

1. **Click** on the **colored title**. A Microsoft Network window will open. In this case, it is Computer Telephony (the fine art of putting a computer in charge of your telephone).

Notice all of the topics related to Computer Telephony. You can visit the chat room at 3:00 P.M. PST and find out how to have your computer screen your calls!

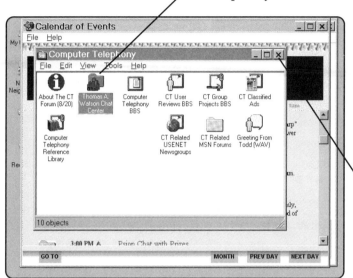

RETURNING TO MSN TODAY

1. Click on the **Close button** ([X]) on the title bar. The Calendar of Events window will reappear.

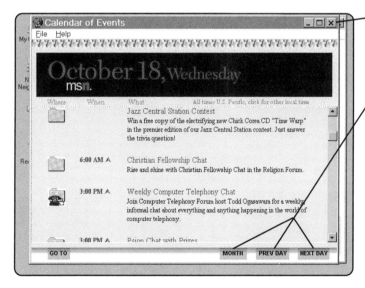

2. Click on the **Close button** ([X]) on the Calendar of Events title bar. The MSN Today window will reappear.

If you want to explore the Calendar of Events a little more before returning to MSN Today, press on the tabs at the bottom right of the Calendar of Events window. They will take you back to the monthly overview or to the event list for the previous or next day.

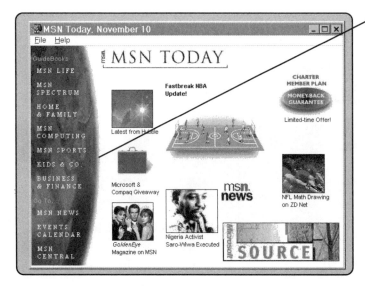

There are several GuideBooks that give you an overview of what's available in MSN, listed on the left side of the MSN Today window. We'll take a closer look at them in the next chapter.

Note: If you want to take a break before continuing, don't forget to sign off the network by following the directions at the end of Chapter 2. Otherwise you'll be paying for your break!

Exploring MSN through GuideBooks

To help you find your way through all that The Microsoft Network has to offer, Microsoft offers GuideBooks. It might be helpful to think of GuideBooks as online magazines that tell you what's available and help you get there. There are several GuideBooks to choose from. In this chapter you will do the following:

✔ Explore the MSN Life GuideBook

✔ Use the "Find" command to search for GuideBooks

✔ Use the "Go to" command to go directly to an MSN location

✔ Use the Windows 95 taskbar to get to the Find and Go to commands

✔ Use the Directory of MSN Areas and Go Words

EXPLORING MSN LIFE

In this section, you will browse MSN's biweekly member magazine.

1. **Open The Microsoft Network** to **MSN Today,** if it isn't already on your screen.

Notice that the MSN Today screen looks different than in the previous chapter. This screen changes daily.

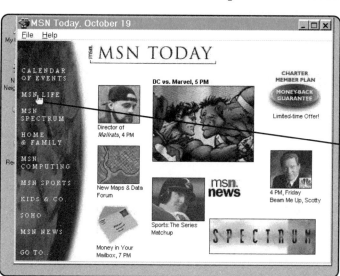

2. **Place** the **mouse arrow** on **MSN LIFE**. The arrow will turn into a hand.

3. **Click** on **MSN LIFE**. The MSN Life window will appear.

Each GuideBook is laid out a little differently, but most share some common elements. For example, most have buttons that help you navigate through the GuideBook. The opening screen, or contents page, of MSN Life has two buttons. The top one takes you to the next page. The bottom one closes the GuideBook.

Reading an Article

The contents page for all GuideBooks includes an overview of what the GuideBook contains. In the case of MSN Life, there is a list of departments for the current issue and a summary of the stories within each department. To read the stories, just click on the name of the department you're interested in. (You can also click on the next page button to begin at the top.)

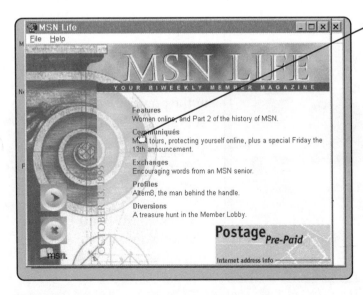

1. **Place** the **mouse arrow** on the **department name**. The pointer will turn into a hand.

2. **Click** on the **department name**. The first story in the department will appear.

Notice that two more navigation buttons have appeared. The top one takes you back to the contents page. The one below the next page button takes you to the previous page. (Each Guide-Book has different buttons with their own look, but all perform the same tasks.)

Just under the name of the department is a list of the stories that appear in this department. The first one is grayed out, telling us that it's the one we're looking at. You can skip to one of the other stories at any time by clicking on the story's name.

3. Click repeatedly on the ▼ to scroll through the rest of the story.

Notice that many stories in MSN Life will include one or more icons. Clicking on these icons will take you to another part of the network that will offer information related to the story. (We'll leave that as an exercise for you rather than demonstrating it here.)

At this point, if you want to continue to the next story you can either click on Next Story, the next page button, or the name of the story at the top of the page.

Let's finish up with MSN Life for now and try another way to access GuideBooks.

1. Click on the **Close button** ($\boxed{\times}$) on the title bar. Repeat this with each window that appears until you are back at the MSN Central window.

SEARCHING FOR GUIDEBOOKS

The Microsoft Network has several ways to access locations on the network. The most useful of these is searching the directory of services.

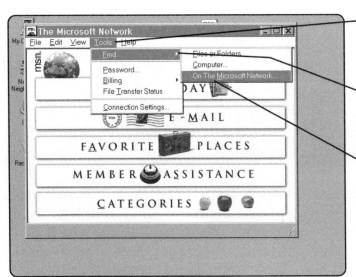

1. Click on **Tools** in the menu bar. The Tools menu will appear.

2. Move the **mouse arrow** down to **Find**. A second menu will appear.

3. Click on **On The Microsoft Network**. The Find window will appear.

We'll be covering the Find window in more detail later in the book, so for now just make sure your settings match the ones shown here.

4. **Type guidebooks** in the text box.

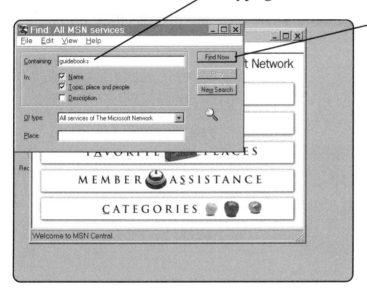

5. **Click** on **Find Now**. The Find window will expand, and the network will begin its search.

Be patient while the network is searching; it has a lot of services to search through! When it's finished, the results will be displayed in the bottom of the Find window.

Four services were found that contained the word "guidebooks." Three are MSN GuideBooks folders and the fourth is a text document describing GuideBooks. (The Type column to the right of the service name will tell you what type of service it is.) Why *three* MSN Guidebooks folders? There are different versions for different countries. We happen to know that the last one is the USA version.

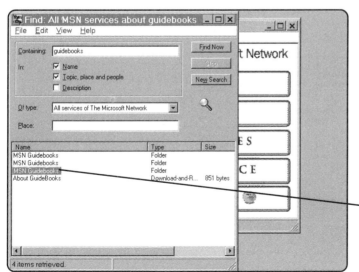

6. **Click twice** on the last MSN GuideBooks entry. The MSN GuideBooks window will appear.

USING THE GO TO COMMAND

To make it easier to get back to a location, MSN offers a Go to command that lets you go directly to any location. First, however, you must know the "Go Word" for that location.

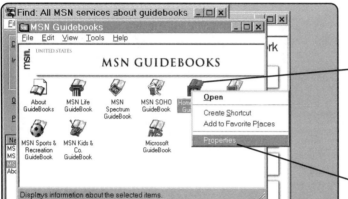

1. Click on the **icon** of the location you're interested in using the **right mouse button**. A pop-up menu will appear.

2. Click on **Properties**. The Properties dialog box will appear.

3. Write down the **Go Word** shown in the Properties dialog box.

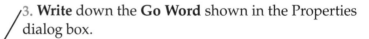

4. Click on the **Close button** ([×]) on the title bar. The MSN GuideBooks window will reappear.

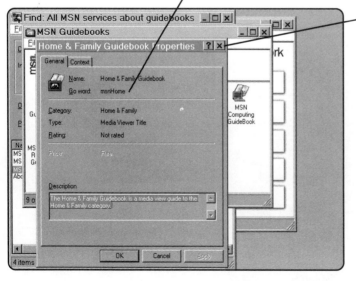

Using the Go Word

Now that you have the right Go Word, you can use it with the Go to command to jump directly to the location from anywhere in the network.

1. Click on **Edit** in the menu bar. The Edit menu will appear.

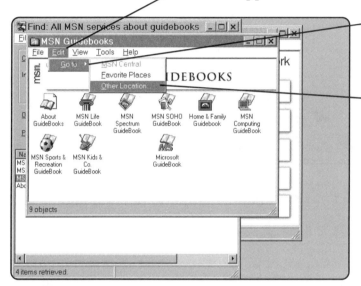

2. Move the **mouse arrow** down to **Go to**. A second menu will appear.

3. Click on **Other Location**. The Go To Service dialog box will appear.

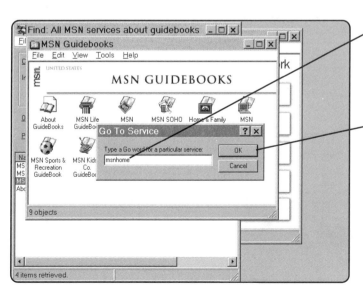

4. Type the **Go Word** you wrote down from the Properties dialog box in the text box.

5. Click on **OK**. The window for the location you specified will appear. (In this case, the Home & Family GuideBook window.)

Notice that the Home & Family GuideBook looks different than the MSN Life Guidebook. But it still has navigation buttons on the left side of the page and a list of stories on the right. (The appearance of the GuideBooks is changed regularly, so what you see may not be the same as what is shown here.) If you would like to explore this GuideBook, you can click on the colored text within the story descriptions, or click on the Next button to go to the first story.

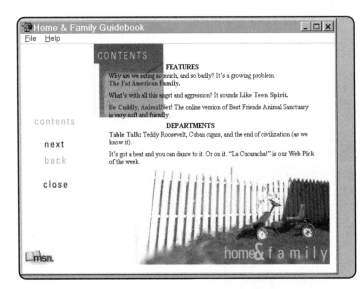

USING THE TASKBAR FOR GO TO AND FIND SEARCHES

In some windows, such as this one, the Edit and Tools menus do not appear. You can still access the Find and Go to commands using a nifty shortcut from the taskbar.

Note: If your taskbar is hidden and you're not sure how to get it back, turn to the Appendix for directions. We have our taskbar set to Auto hide, which makes it invisible until we move the cursor over it.

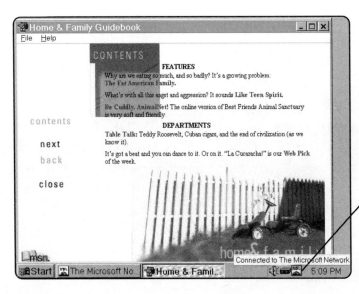

1. **Move** the **mouse arrow** down to the **MSN icon** in the taskbar. The Connected to ... label will appear.

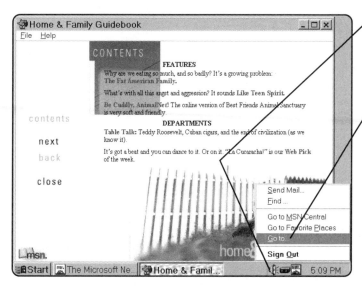

2. Click on the **MSN icon** using the **right mouse button**. A pop-up menu will appear.

3. Click on **Go to**. The Go To Service dialog box will appear.

Notice that Find also appears as an option in the pop-up menu. It is the same as the Find option in the Tools menu.

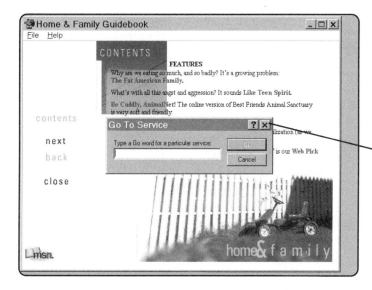

You'll have a chance to use the Go to command some more later in the book. For now, let's look at another shortcut; this one's for going to the Find dialog box.

4. Click on the **Close button** (☒) on the title bar. The Go To Service dialog box will disappear.

USING THE START MENU TO FIND

If you prefer, you can also access the Find menu from the Windows 95 Start menu.

1. **Click** on the **Start button** on the taskbar.

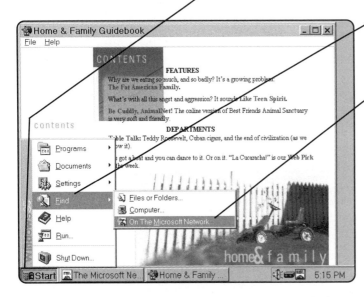

2. **Move** the **mouse arrow** up to **Find**. A second menu will appear.

3. **Click** on **On The Microsoft Network**. The Find window will appear.

You'll probably find yourself using this shortcut a lot, especially while you're exploring the network.

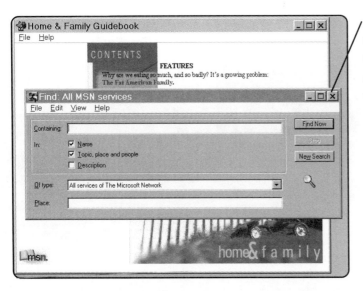

4. **Click** on the **Close button** ([×]) on the title bar. Repeat this with each window that appears until you are back at the MSN Central window.

USING THE GO WORD DIRECTORY

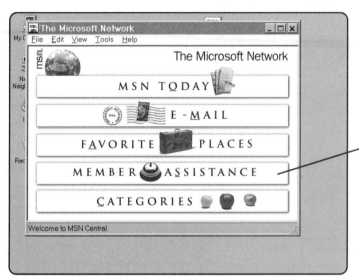

If a handy overview of The Microsoft Network and a list of all the Go Words for the network sounds appealing, you'll love the Directory of MSN Areas and Go Words.

1. **Click** on **MEMBER ASSISTANCE**. The Member Assistance window will appear.

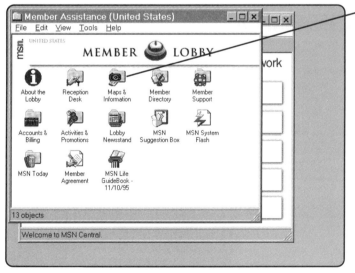

2. **Click twice** on the **Maps & Information icon**. The Maps and Information window will appear.

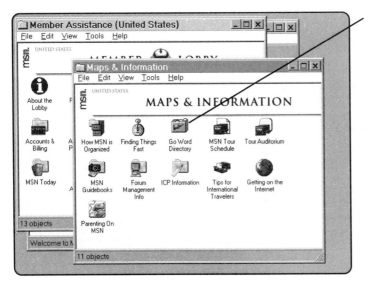

3. **Click twice** on the **Go Word Directory icon**. The Directory of MSN Areas and Go Words will appear.

There are three ways that you can view the information in this directory. The first is alphabetically, which is best if you're looking for a particular area. For a general overview of the network by subject, you can look at the information by category. Finally, if you click on Printable list, you can print either the alphabetical or category list as a handy reference guide. We'll take a look at the category list for this example.

4. **Click** on **By Category**. The right side of the window will display a list of areas in the network arranged by category.

The left column of the list contains the names of the different areas of the network, organized by category. The right column gives the Go Words for each area.

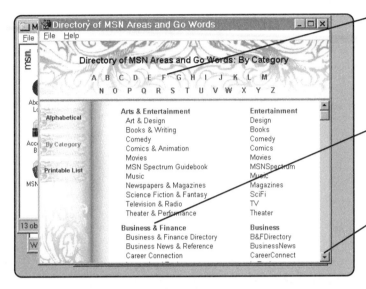

To jump to the categories beginning with a particular letter, click on that letter in the list at the top of the directory.

To jump directly to a category's section in the network, click on the category's name.

To scroll through the list, click repeatedly on the ▼ at the bottom of the scroll bar.

5. **Click** on the **Close button** (☒) on the Directory's title bar. Repeat this with each window that appears until you are back at the MSN Central window.

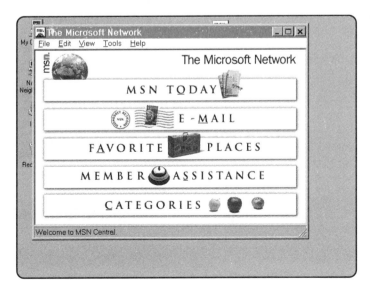

Note: If you want to take a break before going on to the next chapter, don't forget to sign off the network.

Getting Information from Member Assistance

When you need information, it's always nice to know where to go to get it. In The Microsoft Network the place to go for general information about the network is Member Assistance. There you'll find a wealth of resources to help you locate the information you need. In this chapter, you will use these resources to do the following:

✔ Take a guided tour of The Microsoft Network

✔ Create your own personal information profile

✔ Search for information about another member

✔ Check the current charges to your Microsoft Network account

TAKING A GUIDED TOUR

In this section, you will take a guided tour of The Microsoft Network. (It's more of a guided discussion, actually, but Microsoft calls it a guided tour!)

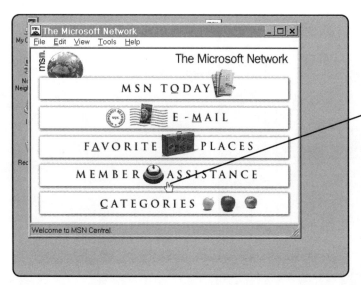

1. **Open The Microsoft Network** to **MSN Central**, if it isn't already on your screen.

2. **Place** the **mouse arrow** on **MEMBER ASSISTANCE**. The arrow will turn into a hand.

3. **Click** on **MEMBER ASSISTANCE**. The Member Assistance window will appear.

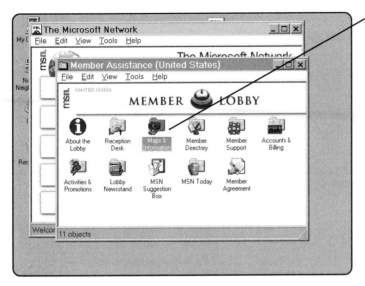

4. Click twice on the **Maps & Information icon**. The Maps & Information window will appear.

Both the Member Lobby and the Maps & Information section have quite a few options to explore. We'll cover many of them in different parts of this book, but you may want to come back afterwards and explore the others on your own.

Checking the Tour Schedule

Tours are held at specific times during the day, so the first thing you need to do is check those times.

1. Click twice on the **MSN Tour Schedule icon**. There will be a short delay, then the schedule will appear on your screen.

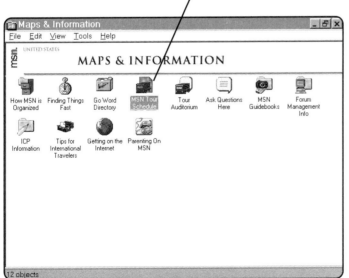

The MSN Tour Schedule is a formatted text document that is sent by the network to your computer. The network will then open the document with Microsoft Word if Word is installed on your computer, or with WordPad if it isn't. The network will automatically run the correct program if it isn't already running.

You can now read through the schedule and find out when the tours will take place and how to get there. At the time this book was written, the tours were given twice a day at 3:00 p.m. and 6:00 p.m., PST. These times may have changed by the time you read this, however, so be sure to check the schedule yourself.

2. Click on the **Close button** ([X]) on the title bar. (If you prefer to keep Word or WordPad open in case you download another file, click on the **Minimize button** ([_]) on the title bar instead.) The Maps & Information window will reappear.

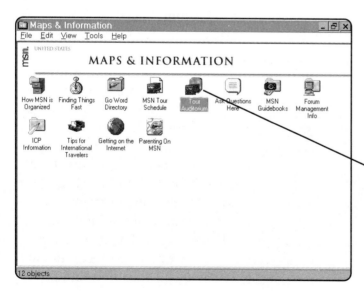

Taking a Tour

Assuming that you have waited until the time shown in the schedule, you are now ready to take the tour.

1. Click twice on the **Tour Auditorium icon**. The Tour Auditorium window will appear.

As you can see from this screen, tours are really nothing more than guided descriptions of different parts of The Microsoft Network. These descriptions are given by Microsoft tour guides. All you have to do is sit back and read what they have to say.

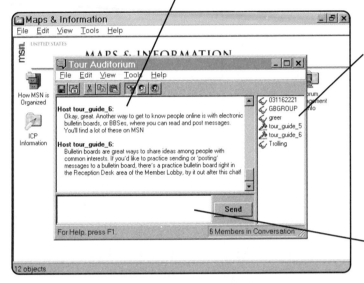

You can see who else is participating in the tour by looking at the list on the right side of the window. A glasses icon to the left of a member ID indicates that the person is a spectator. A gavel icon indicates that the person is a tour guide.

This box is not functional during the tour.

Note: Tours take place in a chat room. For more information on using chat rooms, see the next chapter.

Asking Questions

If you want to ask the tour guides questions to be answered at the end of the tour, you must do so in the Ask Questions Here room.

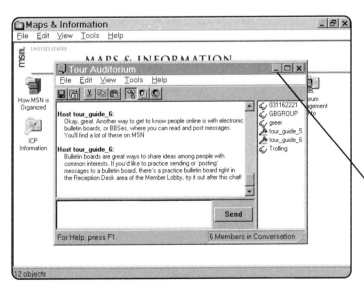

1. Click on the **Minimize button** ([_]) on the title bar. The Maps & Information window will reappear. (We're using minimize so we can come back later.)

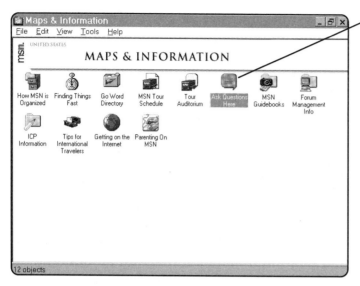

2. Click twice on the **Ask Questions Here icon**. The Ask Questions Here window will open.

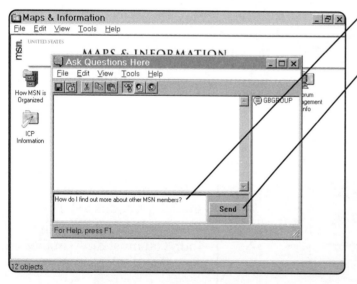

3. Type a **question**. It will appear in the message box.

4. Press the **Enter key** on your keyboard or **Click** on **Send**. Your question will appear in the chat box above the message box.

Your question has now been sent to the tour guides. They will respond to it on a first-come, first-served basis.

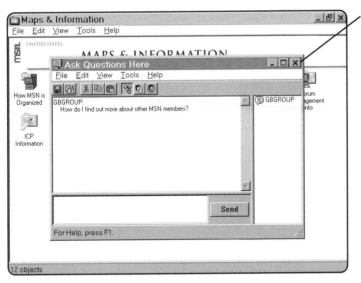

5. **Click** on the **Close button** ([X]) on the title bar. The Maps & Information window will reappear.

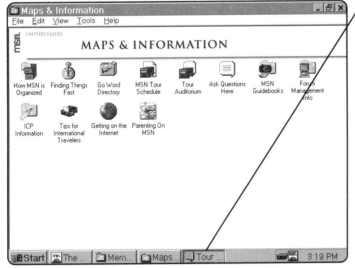

6. **Click** on the **Tour button** in the taskbar. The Tour Auditorium window will reappear. If your taskbar is hidden and you're not sure how to get it back on the screen, turn to the Appendix for directions.

Note: Clicking twice on the Tour Auditorium icon at this point will open a new tour window, not the one you minimized.

Now wait for your question to be answered. (We won't, because we already know the answer!) If you like, you can also use the scroll bar to scroll up and see what you missed while you were typing your question.

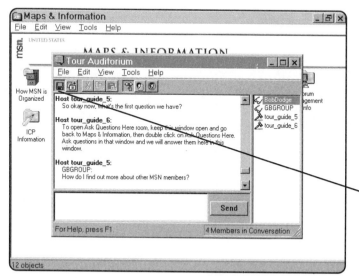

Saving the Tour

Once the tour is over, you may want to save a copy of it so you can refer to it later.

1. **Click** on the **Save button** at the left of the toolbar just below the menu bar. The Save As dialog box will appear.

Use the Save As dialog box to tell the system where to save the tour. We assume you already know how to save a file, but here's a summary just in case!

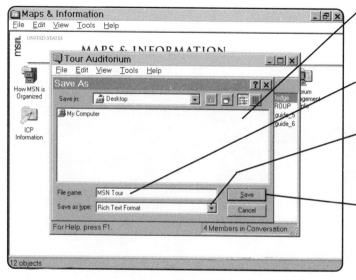

Select a folder by clicking twice on the appropriate items in this box.

Name your tour file by typing a name in this box.

Choose a file type from the pop-up menu that appears when you click on the ▼.

2. **Click** on the **Save button** when you're ready to save the file. The Tour Auditorium window will reappear.

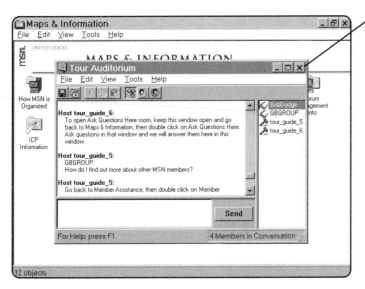

3. Click on the **Close button** ([X]) on the title bar. The Maps & Information window will reappear.

4. Repeat step 3 until the Member Assistance window reappears.

CREATING A PERSONAL PROFILE

You may be curious about the other people who use The Microsoft Network. The network lets you find out more about those people, and you'll see how in a moment. But in order for the network to know anything about its members, each member must first create a personal information profile. (Don't worry—you control how much or how little you want people to know about you.)

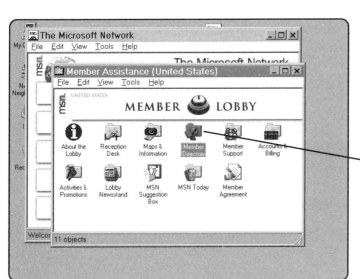

1. Click twice on the **Member Directory icon**. The Member Directory window will appear.

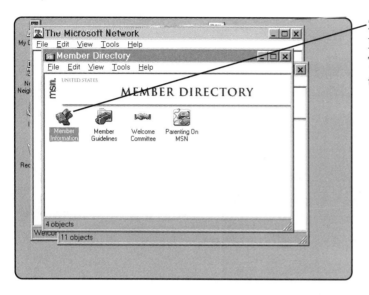

2. Click twice on the **Member Information icon**. The MSN Member Information window will appear.

The MSN Member Information window is divided into two parts. On the left side of the window is a list of topics that you can get information about. On the right side of the window is the information you have requested.

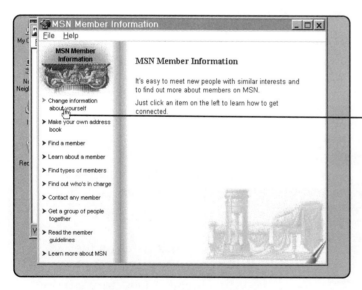

3. Click on **Change information about yourself**. The instructions on how to change your information will appear on the right side of the window.

As you can see on this screen, there are several steps you need to take to create a profile for yourself. Fortunately, we'll be going over them all in the next few pages, so you don't need to write any of them down!

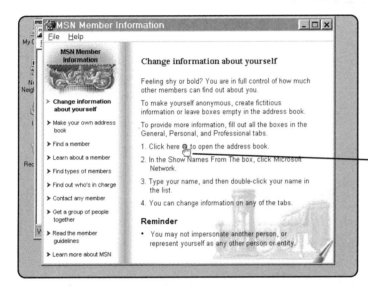

Finding Yourself

The first step to creating a personal profile is to find yourself in the Microsoft Network address book.

1. Click on the **blue star icon.** Microsoft Exchange will open in a new window. (It may take a few seconds.)

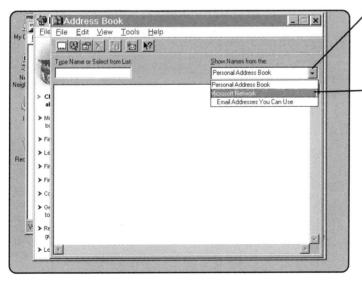

2. Click on the ▼ to the right of Personal Address Book. A pop-up menu will appear.

3. Click on **Microsoft Network.** A list of Microsoft Network member names will appear in the lower part of the window.

4. **Click** in the **upper left box** to place the cursor.

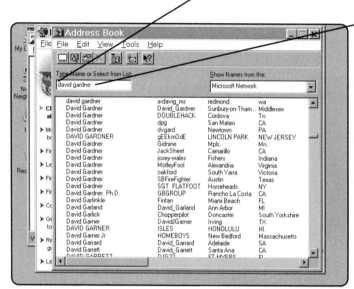

5. **Start typing your name**. The list of member names will change as you type to display those names that match what you've typed so far. You only need to type enough of your name so that you can see your name and member ID in the list.

Note: Several other people may have the same first and last name as you. Make sure that you see your member ID next to your name.

Entering Your Information

Now that you've found yourself in the address book, you can enter the information in your profile.

1. **Click twice** on **your member ID**. The Properties dialog box will appear.

(You could also click twice on your name, but clicking on the member ID makes sure you don't accidentally select someone else with the same name.)

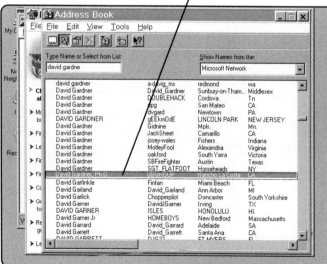

You can now type in the information you would like other people to know about you. Use the tab key to move between text boxes.

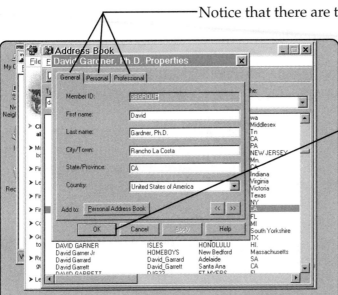

Notice that there are three tabs at the top of the Properties dialog box. Click on each tab to enter general, personal, and professional information about yourself.

2. **Click** on **OK** when you're done. The Address Book window will reappear.

FINDING ANOTHER MEMBER

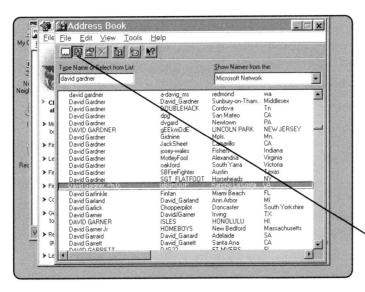

You can use the address book to get information about another network member or to find members that match certain criteria (all the members from your hometown who work in your profession, for example). Finding a member is just as easy as entering your personal profile.

1. **Click** on the **Find button** below the menu bar. The Find dialog box will appear.

Notice that the Find dialog box looks just like the Properties dialog box. You'll enter the same type of information you used to fill in your profile. This time, however, the network will use that information to find members with identical information in *their* profiles.

Don't forget to use the tabs at the top of the window to access the different information areas.

2. **Click** in the **box** you want to use for your search. In this case, we'll search for a member ID we saw in a MSN Life article. You can search for our member ID (GBGROUP) if you'd like.

3. **Type** the **text** you want to search for.

4. **Repeat steps 2 and 3** until you have entered all the information you want to search for.

5. **Click** on **OK**. The network will begin its search. When it's done (it may take a few seconds) the Address Book window will reappear with a list of members that match the information you specified.

Note: If you do enter information in more than one box, the network will search for members whose profiles match *all* of the information you entered. So, for example, if you enter a last name and a city the network will find only those members who have that last name *and* live in that city.

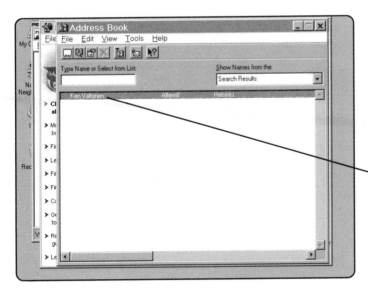

Since we searched for a specific member, the network only found that member. Depending on what you search for, you may end up with several or many members on your screen.

6. **Click twice** on the **member** you want to know more about. The Properties dialog box for that member will appear.

Once again, you can click on the tabs at the top of the window to review the different types of information the member has entered into his or her personal profile.

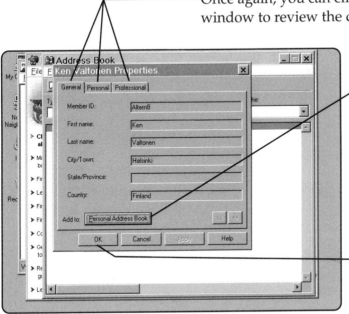

If you would like to add this member to your personal address book so you can easily send e-mail to him or her in the future, click on the Personal Address Book button near the bottom of the window.

7. **Click** on **OK**. The Address Book window will reappear.

Notice that you can also add a member to your personal address book from your search results by clicking on the member name and then clicking on the Add to Personal Address Book icon at the top of the window.

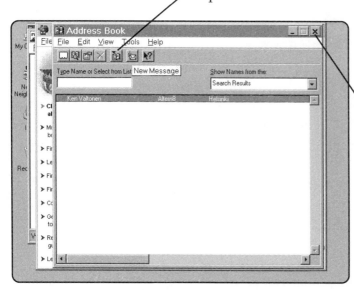

8. Click on the **Close button** ([X]) on the title bar. Repeat this with each window that appears until you are back at the Member Assistance window.

CHECKING YOUR ACCOUNT

It's easy to lose track of time while you explore The Microsoft Network. Since you're being charged for your time, however, it's nice to be able to check your account balance from time to time and avoid end of the month surprises! In this section, you'll learn how to check your account balance online.

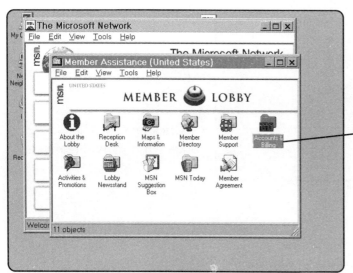

1. Click twice on the **Accounts & Billing icon**. The Accounts & Billing window will appear.

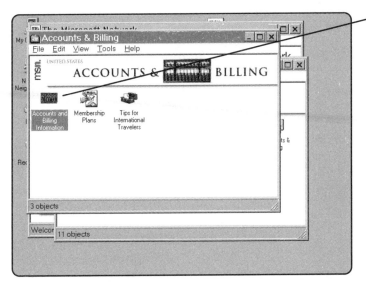

2. **Click twice** on the **Accounts and Billing Information icon**. The Accounts & Billing Frequently Asked Questions window will appear.

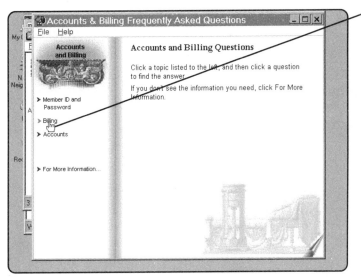

3. **Click** on **Billing**. A list of billing questions will appear on the right side of the window.

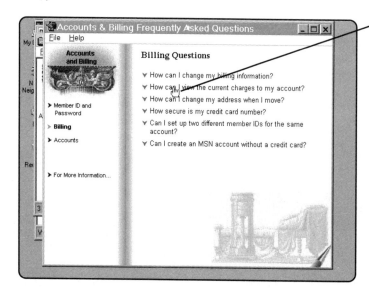

4. **Click** on **How can I view the current charges to my account?** An explanation of how to view your charges will appear on the right side of the window.

We'll actually walk you through this process over the next few pages, but we wanted to show you how you can look for this type of information within the network. Remember that we started from the Member Assistance window, which is always the first place to turn when you're stuck.

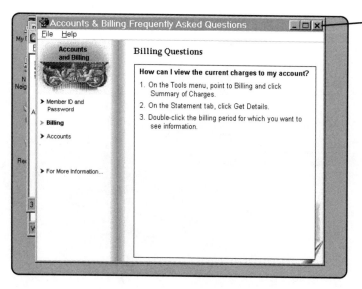

5. **Click** on the **Close buttons** ([X]) on the title bars of this and the previous screen so that the Accounts & Billing window reappears.

Viewing the Summary of Charges

Now that you've found out how to view the current charges to your account, you can go ahead and try it. (If you dare!)

1. **Click** on **Tools** in the menu bar. The Tools menu will appear.

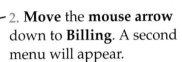
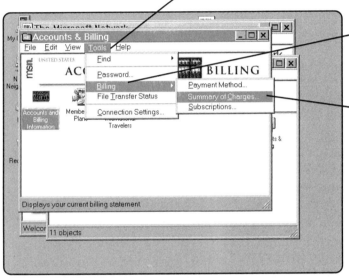

2. **Move** the **mouse arrow** down to **Billing**. A second menu will appear.

3. **Click** on **Summary of Charges**. The Online Statement dialog box will appear.

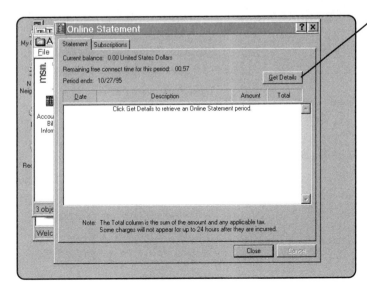

4. **Click** on the **Get Details button**. The Get Details dialog box will appear.

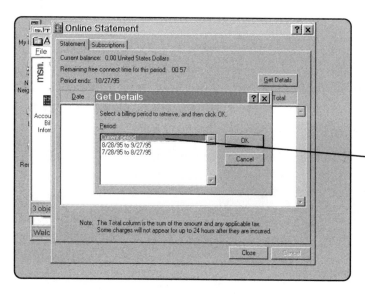

The Get Details dialog box will give you a choice of billing periods that you can look at. For this example, we want to see the current period.

5. **Click twice** on **Current Period**. The Online Statement dialog box will reappear showing the current statement of charges.

You can also review a statement for any services you subscribe to within the network by clicking on the Subscriptions tab at the top of the window.

You can get more information on a particular charge by clicking twice on it. (This is the same as clicking once and then clicking on the Get Details button.)

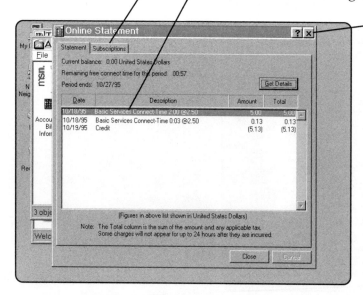

6. **Click** on the **Close button** ([X]) on the title bar. Repeat this with each window that appears until you are back at the MSN Central window.

We've covered a lot of material, and you may want to take a well-deserved rest before continuing to the next chapter. If so, remember to sign off. Otherwise you might be in for a shock the next time you go to review your charges!

The Microsoft Network

Part IV: Having Fun

Meeting People and Chatting in Forums

You've probably heard about couples who meet online and end up dating and eventually marrying. Even if you've already found the love of your life and aren't interested in a romance connection, The Microsoft Network is a great place to meet interesting people. In this chapter, you will do the following:

✔ Look for interesting conversations

✔ Join a conversation

✔ Customize a chat room

✔ Use a shortcut to get to different chat rooms

FINDING A CONVERSATION

As you'll soon see, chatting with other members on The Microsoft Network is a lot like chatting with other people in person. The first thing you need to do is find a conversation to join.

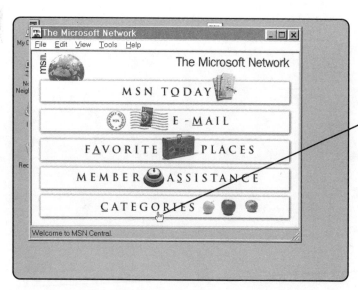

1. **Open The Microsoft Network** to **MSN Central**, if it isn't already on your screen.

2. **Click** on **CATEGORIES**. The Categories window will appear.

Making Room

In a window like this, where there are a lot of icons, the window may not be big enough to show them all. You can use the scroll bar on the right side of the window to scroll down, but you may prefer to make the window a little bigger instead.

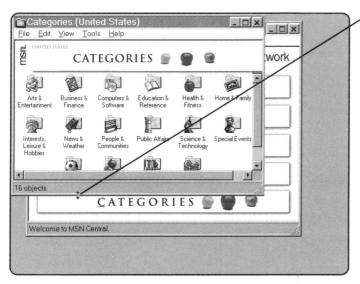

1. **Move** the **mouse arrow** over the bottom or right edge, or over the lower-right corner of the window. The arrow will change into a two-headed arrow.

2. **Press and hold** the **mouse button** as you **drag** the edge or corner of the window down or to the right.

3. **Release** the **mouse button** when the window is the size that you want.

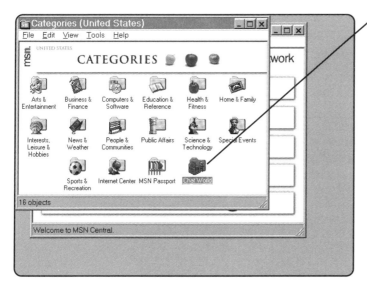

4. **Click twice** on the **Chat World icon**. The Chat World window will appear.

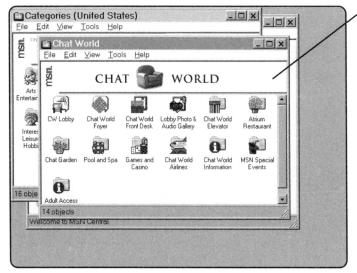

Chat World is set up to resemble a grand hotel, and most of the icons you see in the Chat World window will take you to different areas of the hotel that you can use for conversations. You can browse through these areas if you like and hope to stumble across a conversation in progress. Your best bet, however, is to start out in the Lobby or Foyer, where most people gather when they first enter Chat World.

Reviewing the Guidelines

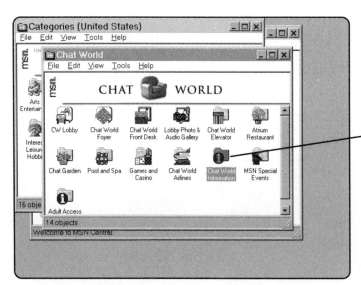

If this is your first time in Chat World, you should review the Chat World guidelines before entering the Lobby.

1. **Click twice** on the **Chat World Information icon**. The Chat World Information window will appear.

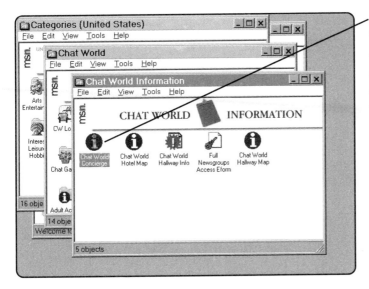

2. **Click twice** on the **Chat World Concierge icon.** There will be a short delay while the network sends the file to your computer and opens up Microsoft Word or WordPad to view it. The document will then appear on your screen.

This document is an introduction to Chat World and the guidelines that apply to using it. Make sure you read it and that you follow these guidelines when participating in conversations. It will make everyone's online chat experience a lot more enjoyable!

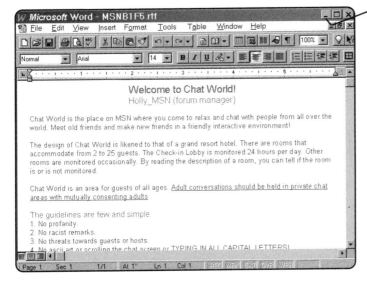

3. **Click** on the **Minimize button** ([_]) on the title bar when you're finished. (We'll be looking at another file later in the chapter, so we may as well minimize the window instead of closing the program.)

4. **Click** on the **Close button** ([x]) on the title bar of the Chat World Information window when it reappears. The Chat World window will reappear.

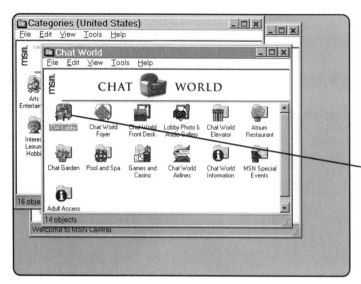

Entering the Lobby

Now you're ready to enter the Lobby. Take a deep breath and get your fingers ready!

1. Click twice on the **CW Lobby icon**. A message will appear telling you that Chat is starting. Then one of two different windows will appear. We'll show you both.

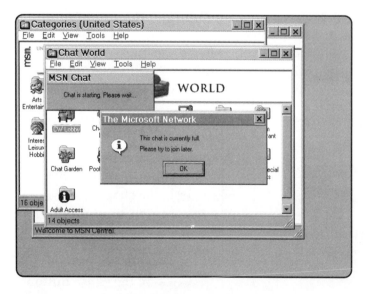

Both the Lobby and the Foyer can only hold 35 people at a time. (Other rooms in Chat World are designed to hold from 2 to 25 people. The room name usually tells you how many.) If a room is full when you try to enter it, a dialog box will appear like the one shown here, telling you to try again later. If this happens, click on the OK button and either try again or try a different room.

Once there's enough room for you in the Lobby (people come and go all the time, so it shouldn't take too long), the CW Lobby window will appear. Shortly after it does, you'll see a message from the room's host welcoming you.

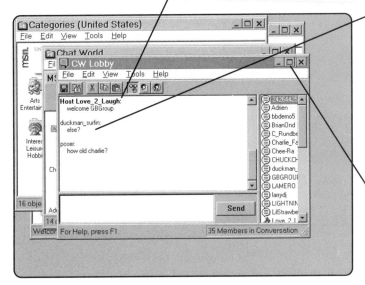

Pretty soon you'll start to see conversations on your screen between the people already in the room.

There's a lot going on in a chat window, so it helps to make it as large as possible.

2. **Click** on the **Maximize button** (□) on the title bar. The window will resize to fill the screen.

JOINING THE CONVERSATION

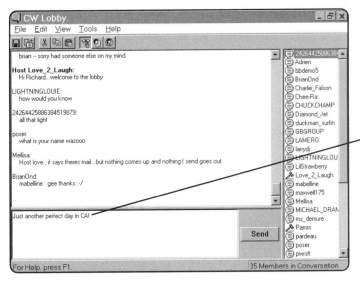

You need reasonable typing skills and the ability to say what you want as concisely as possible if you want to participate effectively in chat area discussions.

1. The cursor will already be flashing in the message box, so **type** your **message**.

2. **Press Enter on your keyboard** (or click on Send). Your message will appear in the chat box.

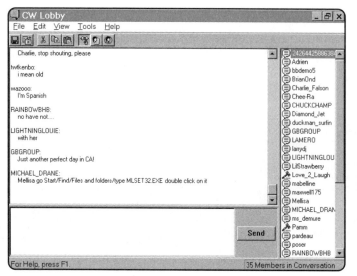

Many conversations are going on at once in most chat rooms, especially in the Lobby and Foyer. As a result, if you respond to something someone else has said, your response may not appear directly below that person's comment or question. It may also take a while for the other person to respond to your reply, so be patient. It does take a minute to get the hang of a busy room.

Checking People Out

The list of member IDs on the right side of the chat window shows who's in this room. A speech balloon icon next to an ID shows that the member is participating in the chat. A pair of glasses indicates that the person is a spectator and cannot participate

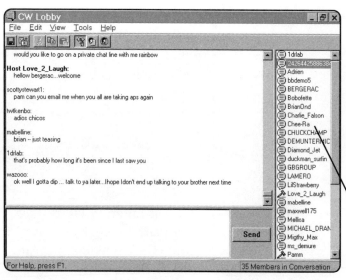

in the chat, while a gavel indicates that the person is a room host. (Hosts are in charge of helping out and making sure everyone follows the guidelines.)

If you want to know something about any member in a room, you can look at that person's profile.

1. **Click twice** on the **person's member ID**. The Member properties dialog box will appear.

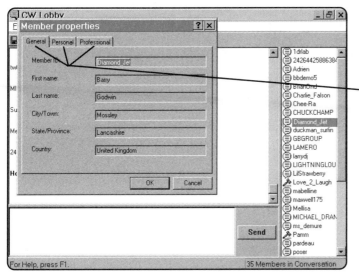

You should recognize the general look of this window from the previous chapter.

You can click on the tabs at the top of the window to look at the different types of information in this member's profile.

2. **Click** on the **Close button** ([X]) on the title bar. The CW Lobby window will reappear.

Ignoring the Obnoxious

Unfortunately, not all members are charming chat companions. If someone is being obnoxious, you can stop their messages from appearing on your screen. (Official disclaimer: This is only an example and is in no way meant to imply that BrianOnd is obnoxious!)

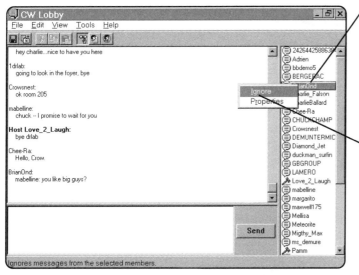

1. In the list of member IDs at the right side of the window, **click** the **right mouse button** on the **Member ID** of the person you want to ignore. A pop-up menu will appear.

2. **Click** on **Ignore**. That member's comments will no longer appear in your chat box. (Other members will still be able to see and respond to the member's comments, however.)

Leaving a Chat Room

If you have actually been involved in the conversation in a chat room, it's polite to tell people you're leaving.

1. **Type** your **farewell message**. It will appear in the message box.

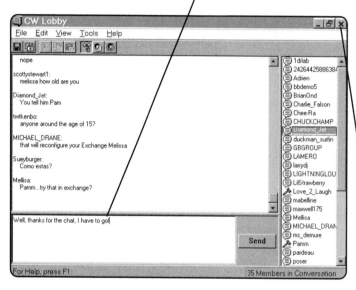

2. **Press Enter on your keyboard** (or click on Send). Your message will appear in the chat box.

You may want to wait for people to say goodbye.

3. **Click** on the **Close box** ([X]) on the title bar. The Chat World window will reappear.

CUSTOMIZING CHAT AREAS

There are several ways you can control the environment in a chat room. We'll start by making the chat box bigger so we can follow the conversation more easily. Go back to the Lobby (or any other chat room) to try this.

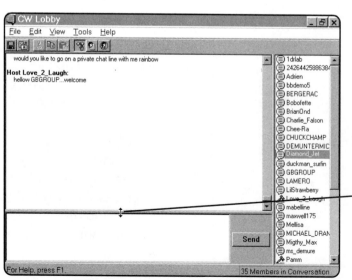

1. **Move** the **mouse arrow** over the bar between the chat box and the message box. The arrow will change into a two-headed arrow.

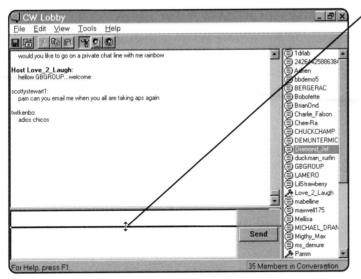

2. **Click and drag** the bar down until the message box is the size you want it.

3. **Release** the **mouse button**. The chat box and message box will resize themselves accordingly.

Setting Chat Options

There are several options you can set for a chat room, all accessible from the Options dialog box.

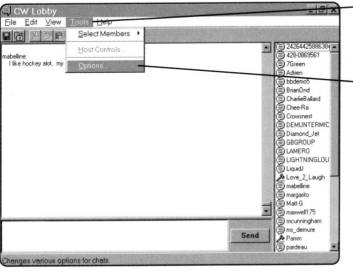

1. **Click** on **Tools** in the menu bar. The Tools menu will appear.

2. **Click** on **Options**. The Options dialog box will appear.

The options available in this window should be self-explanatory. Click on an option to put a ✔ in the box next to it. This will turn the option on. If a ✔ is already in the box, click on it to turn the option off.

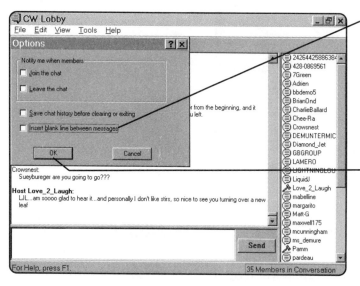

3. For example, **click** on **"Insert blank line between messages."** A ✔ will appear in the box next to it or disappear if one was already there. In our case we turned the option off.

4. **Click** on **OK**. The CW Lobby window will reappear and the option change will take effect.

As you can see, this option gets rid of the blank lines between each member's message. This gives you more time to read each message before it scrolls off the screen. (Of course, you can always use the scroll bar to scroll back up and read something you missed.)

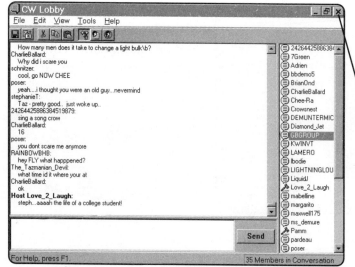

5. **Click** on the **Close button** ([✕]) on the title bar. The Chat World window will reappear.

EXPLORING OTHER CHAT ROOMS

There are dozens of chat rooms to explore in Chat World, all of which are smaller than the Lobby and Foyer and therefore much more amenable to more personal conversations. While you can explore these rooms by looking through each of the Chat World folders, there is a nifty way to get to them more quickly. In this section, you'll use this shortcut to get to one of these rooms.

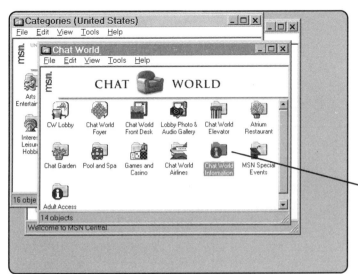

1. Click twice on the **Chat World Information icon**. The Chat World Information window will appear.

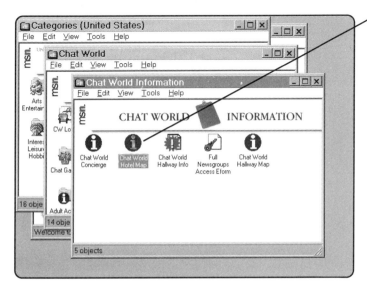

2. Click twice on the **Chat World Hotel Map icon**. A Downloading window will appear while the network sends the Chat World Hotel Map file to your computer.

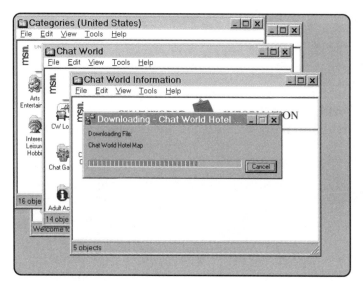

The Chat World Hotel Map is a very large file, so it will take a minute or two for the network to send it. Once it's done, the file will open in either Microsoft Word or WordPad. This process will also take a minute or so, during which you will see a progress bar at the lower left of the program window. Be patient; it's worth the wait!

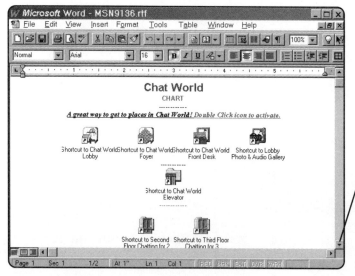

The Chat World Hotel Map gives you a visual overview of the main chat rooms in Chat World. Folder icons represent groups of rooms with similar themes, while plain icons represent individual rooms.

3. **Click repeatedly** on the ▼ at the bottom of the right scroll bar to scroll down to a folder that looks interesting to you.

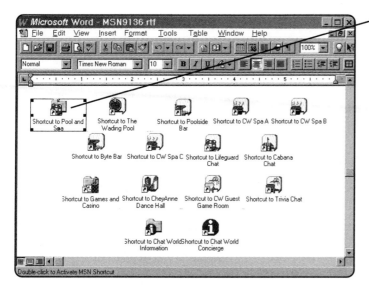

4. Click twice on the **folder icon** of the group you want to go to. The Microsoft Network window for that group will appear.

Getting a Description of a Chat Room

Each chat room is set up for a certain number of people and for a particular type of conversation. You can find out more about a room by checking its Properties dialog box.

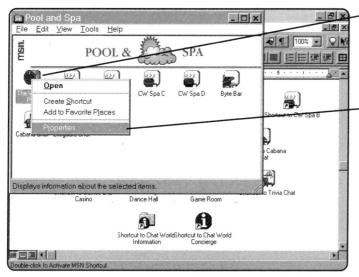

1. Click on a **chat room icon** using the **right mouse button**. A pop-up menu will appear.

2. Click on **Properties**. The Properties dialog box for that room will appear.

There are four main pieces of information you can glean from the room Properties dialog box.

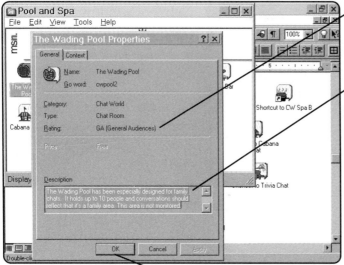

The Rating tells you what type of audience the room is designed for.

The Description box tells you the topic of conversation the room is designed for, how many people the room will hold, and whether or not the room is monitored by a Host. With the exception of the Lobby and the Foyer, different chat rooms will hold anywhere from 2 to 25 people.

3. **Click** on **OK**. The group window will reappear.

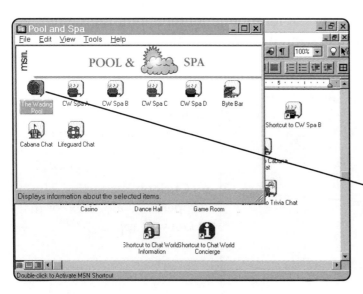

Checking a Room

Unfortunately, there is no way to find out if a room contains any people without actually entering the room.

1. **Click twice** on a **chat room icon**. The room window will appear.

A quick look at the member ID list on the right side of the window will tell you if anyone else is in the room. (So will conversation appearing in the chat box, of course!)

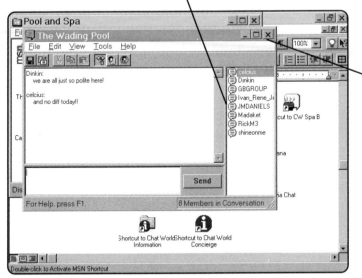

2. When you're finished, **click** on the **Close button** ([X]) on the title bar. (Don't forget to say goodbye if you've been chatting.) Repeat this with the group window. The Microsoft Word or WordPad window will reappear.

Note: If you like the Chat World map, you may want to save it to disk so you don't have to wait (and pay) for it to download again. To do so, click on the Save icon on the toolbar at the top of the screen (or select Save from the File menu).

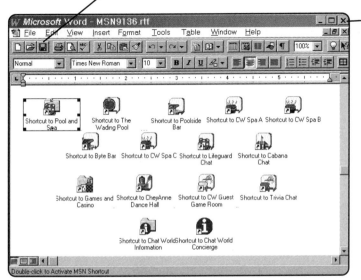

3. **Click** on the **Close button** on the title bar. Repeat this with each window that appears until you are back at the MSN Central window.

If you'll be taking a break before going on to the next chapter, don't forget to sign off the network first. We promise this is the last time we'll remind you!

Using Forums and BBSs

A Microsoft Network forum combines a variety of different services, such as online chatting, bulletin boards (BBSs), informative documents, and files all in one place. Forums are set up around specific topics. These topics include Exercise & Physical Fitness, Personal Investing, Travel, Religion, and many more. In this chapter, you will do the following:

✔ Learn how to find forums

✔ Learn how to use BBSs to exchange messages

FINDING A FORUM

There are several ways to get to forums, but the easiest and most organized way is through the categories area.

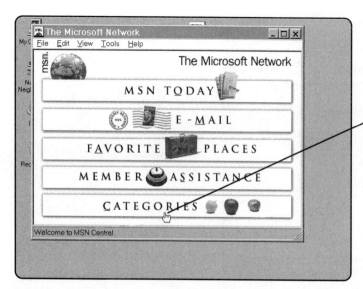

1. Open The Microsoft Network to **MSN Central**, if it isn't already on your screen.

2. Click on **CATEGORIES**. The Categories window will appear.

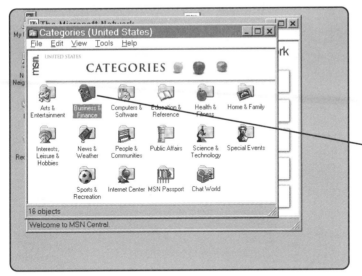

The Categories window organizes the forums into general categories. Within each category are a variety of different forums and subcategories to explore.

3. **Click twice** on the **Business & Finance icon**. The Business and Finance window will appear.

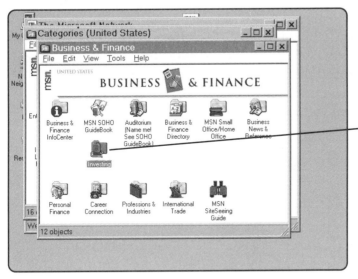

As you get deeper into the heart of a category, you'll start to see more resources appear along with more specific subcategories.

4. **Click twice** on the **Investing icon**. The Investing window will appear.

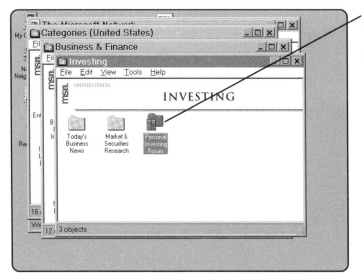

5. **Click twice** on the **Personal Investing Forum icon**. The Personal Investing Forum window will appear.

As you can see, there are several types of resources available to you within a forum. (Not all forums will have the same resources.) The most common are chat areas, software libraries, and BBSs. You learned how to use chat areas in the previous chapter, and we'll cover software libraries in Chapter 13. Let's take a look here at BBSs.

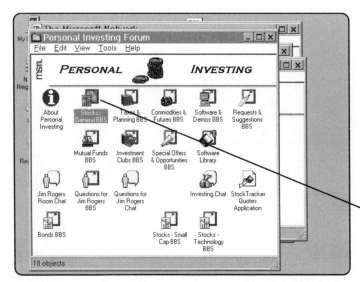

USING A BBS

BBS stands for *Bulletin Board System* and functions like a message center. You can use it to ask questions and receive answers on specific topics from other Microsoft Network members.

1. **Click twice** on the **Stocks-General BBS icon** (or any other BBS icon). The BBS window will appear.

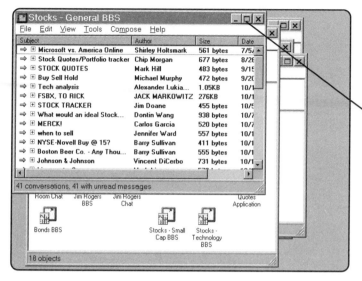

There is a lot of information in a BBS window, so it helps to have the window as large as possible.

2. Click on the **Maximize button** (□) on the title bar. The window will resize to fill the screen.

The BBS window may appear a little overwhelming at first, but it's not as bad as it looks.

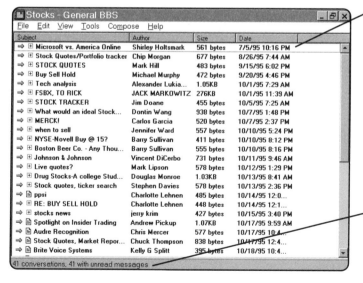

Each line in the BBS window represents a particular topic of conversation. A ➡ icon to the left of a line means you have not read that topic yet. A 🖹 indicates a single message, while a ⊞ means the topic is a conversation, containing more than one message.

The status bar at the bottom of the window tells you how many entries are in the BBS and how many are still unread (by you).

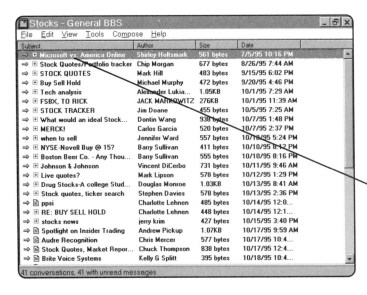

Reading Messages

1. Click on the ▼ at the bottom of the right scroll bar to scroll through the list of topics.

2. Click twice on a **topic** that interests you. A message window will appear with the first message for that topic.

Navigating through Messages

There are several buttons in the toolbar at the top of the message window that help you navigate through the BBS:

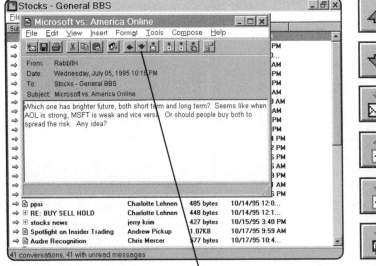

 Opens the previous message

 Opens the next message

 Skips to the next unread message

 Skips to the previous conversation

 Skips to the next conversation

 Skips to the next unread conversation

1. Click on the **Next Message button**. The next message will appear.

Posting a Message

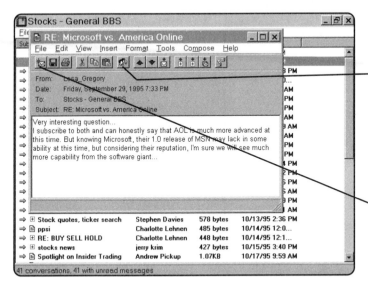

You can reply to a message or start a new topic.

1. To reply to the current message, **click** on the **Reply to BBS button** in the toolbar near the top of the window. A New Message window will appear.

If you want to start a new topic, click on the New Message button instead.

Note: Composing a BBS message is a lot like composing an e-mail message. You may want to review Chapter 4.

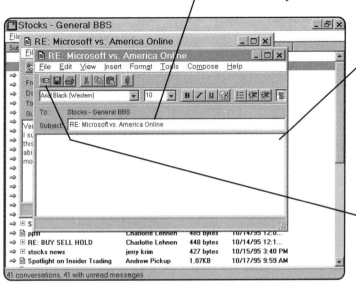

If you are replying to a message, the network will automatically enter a subject for you. To change it, click in the subject box and type a new subject.

Click in the message box and type your message.

If you want, use the formatting tools to format your message and/or add graphics.

Click on the Send button in the toolbar to post your message to the BBS.

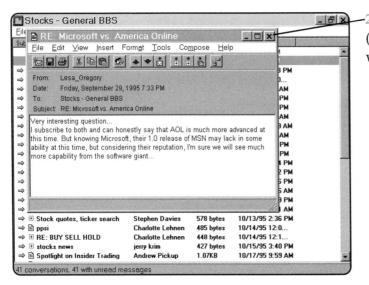

2. Click on the **Close button** ([×]) on the title bar. The BBS window will reappear.

Notice that the BBS window has changed slightly. First, the conversation we were reading has been expanded to show the messages it contains. (You can expand and collapse a conversation at any time by clicking on the ⊞ icon next to it.) Second, the ⇒ icon has been removed from the two messages we read and their descriptions are no longer shown in boldface, indicating that they have been read by you.

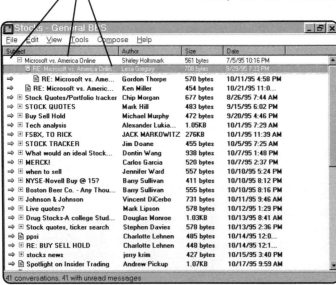

Rearranging Messages

When you first open a forum, the messages in it are arranged by the date of the original message and organized into conversations. If you're trying to find a particular message, you may prefer to arrange them differently.

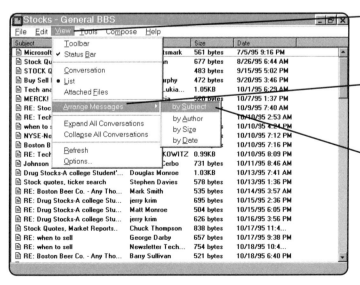

1. **Click** on **View** in the menu bar. The View menu will appear.

2. **Click** on **List**. The BBS will be rearranged so that each message appears on its own line, ordered by date. In other words, messages will no longer be organized into conversations.

Now that you have the messages listed separately, it's no longer useful to have them ordered by date.

3. **Click** on **View** in the menu bar. The View menu will appear.

4. **Move** the **mouse arrow** down to **Arrange Messages**. A second menu will appear.

5. **Click** on **by Subject**. The BBS will be rearranged so the messages are arranged in alphabetical order according to subject.

LEAVING THE FORUM

You may want to spend a little time browsing through the BBS and experimenting with what you've learned in this chapter before leaving the forum. It will be time well spent!

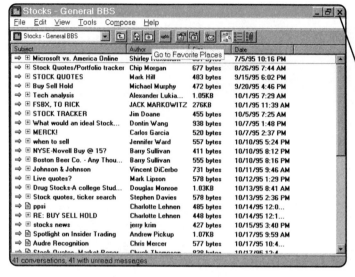

1. **Click** on the **Close button** ([X]) on the title bar. Repeat this with each window that appears until you are back at the MSN Central window.

Shopping on The Microsoft Network

Shopping on The Microsoft Network can save you time, money, and miles of walking at the mall. With the network's shopping locations you can browse through a variety of items in the privacy of your home or office and then e-mail your order when you've decided what you want. All this without leaving the comfort of your keyboard! In this chapter, you will do the following:

✔ Search for The Microsoft Network's shopping services

✔ Browse through several online stores

✔ Learn how to place an order

GOING SHOPPING

The list of shopping services available on The Microsoft Network is constantly changing, so the best way to see what's currently available is to use Find.

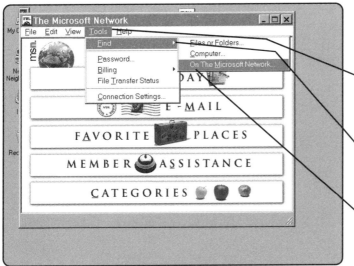

1. **Open The Microsoft Network** to **MSN Central**, if it isn't already on your screen.

2. **Click** on **Tools** in the menu bar. The Tools menu will appear.

3. **Move** the **mouse arrow** down to **Find**. A second menu will appear.

4. **Click** on **On The Microsoft Network**. The Find window will appear.

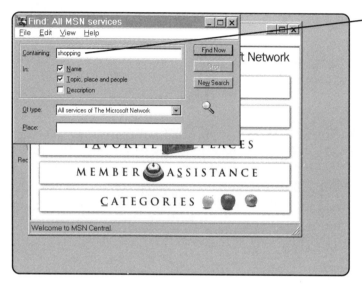

5. **Type shopping** in the Containing box.

6. **Press Enter** on your keyboard (or click on Find Now). The Find window will expand, and the network will begin its search. When it's finished, the results will be displayed in the bottom of the window.

Note: As you can see, there are a variety of shopping services to choose from. Unfortunately, you'll find that some of these services are designed for other countries, such as Germany and Australia. You'll have to do some exploring to find out which ones are which.

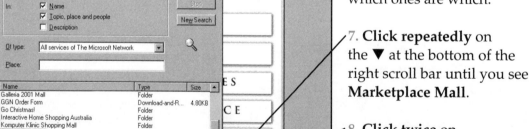

7. **Click repeatedly** on the ▼ at the bottom of the right scroll bar until you see **Marketplace Mall**.

8. **Click twice** on **Marketplace Mall**. The Marketplace Mall window will appear.

BROWSING ONLINE STORES

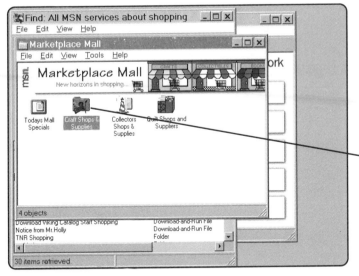

Let's take a look at what some online stores have to offer.

1. Click twice on the **Craft Shops & Supplies icon**. The Craft Shops & Supplies window will appear.

Note: Online services such as The Microsoft Network are constantly changing. New areas are added, and old ones are deleted or moved to other areas every day. The screens that you see on your computer may not be exactly the same as the ones shown here. If you don't see the same online stores we used in these examples, follow along using one that interests you.

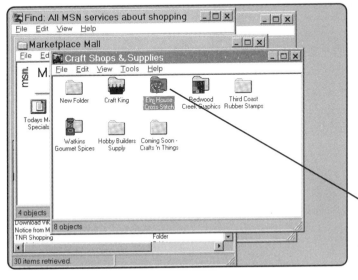

This particular service offers a variety of stores that deal mostly with craft products.

2. Click twice on the **Elm House Cross Stitch icon**. The Elm House Cross Stitch window will appear.

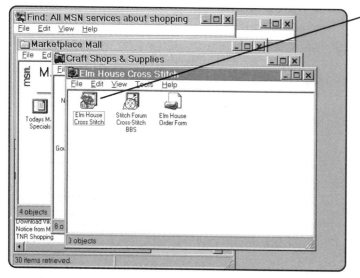

3. Click twice on the **Elm House Cross Stitch icon**. A second Elm House Cross Stitch window will appear.

If you read the previous chapter on BBSs, you probably recognize this as a BBS window. Different stores use different types of windows to sell their wares.

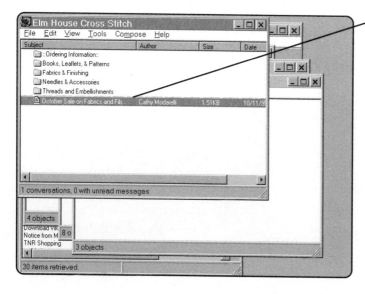

4. Click twice on **October Sale on Fabrics....** After a brief delay a message window will appear.

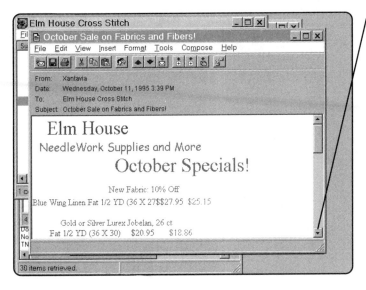

5. **Click repeatedly** on the ▼ at the bottom of the scroll bar. The product descriptions will come into view.

This store uses text to describe its products. Other stores are more picturesque, as we'll see in our next example.

6. **Click** on the **Close button** (⊠) on the title bar. Repeat this with each window that appears until you are back at the Find window.

Searching for Something More

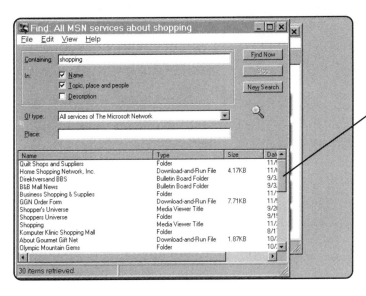

Sometimes the results of a find may not give you everything you want but may hint at a different direction to try.

1. **Drag** the **right scroll box** to the top of the scroll bar.

You should see About Gourmet Gift Net on the list. Gourmet Gift Net itself, however, does not appear on the list.

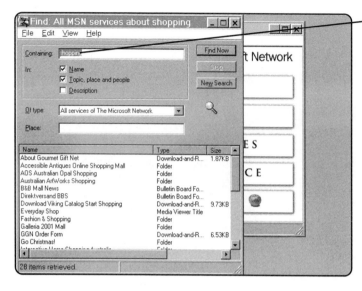

2. Click twice on **shopping** in the Containing box. Shopping will appear highlighted.

3. Type gourmet.

4. Press Enter on your keyboard (or click on Find Now). The network will begin a new search. When it's finished, the new results will be displayed in the bottom of the window.

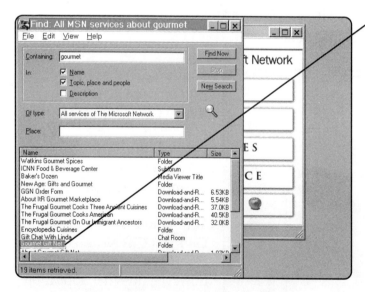

5. Click twice on **Gourmet Gift Net**. The Gourmet Gift Net window will appear.

(If you don't see Gourmet Gift Net in the list at the bottom of the window, click on the ▼ at the bottom of the right scroll bar until it appears.)

Gourmet Gift Net's main window is organized a little differently than the Marketplace Mall, but by now you should know your way around the network well enough to figure out what to do.

6. **Click twice** on the **Sweet Decadence icon** (or any other similar icon). The Online Viewer window will appear briefly, then the Sweet Decadence window will appear.

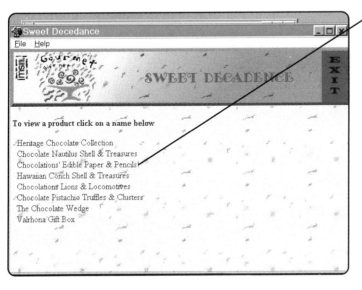

7. **Click** on **Chocolations Edible Paper & Pencils** (yum!). Another Sweet Decadence screen will appear.

Placing an Order

This looks good, so let's assume we want to place an order. (We'll stop short of actually sending the order in, so don't be afraid to continue!)

We first need to scroll down to see the rest of the page before we click on the Order Here button.

1. **Click repeatedly** on the ▼ at the bottom of the right scroll bar until you reach the bottom of the page.

If you really want to place an order, you'll need to make a note of the product number, the price, and the product name.

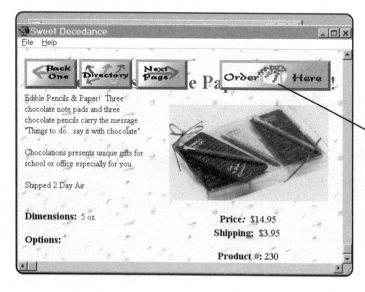

2. **Click** on the **Order Here button**. The network will send the order form to your computer and open it with Microsoft Word or WordPad.

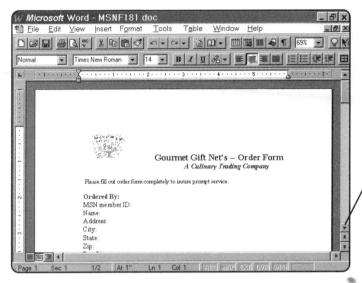

Different companies use various methods to have you place an order. Some, such as this one, use forms that you fill in and then e-mail to them. Others prefer to make money the old-fashioned way—by phone!

3. **Click repeatedly** on the ▼ at the bottom of the right scroll bar until you reach the bottom of the form.

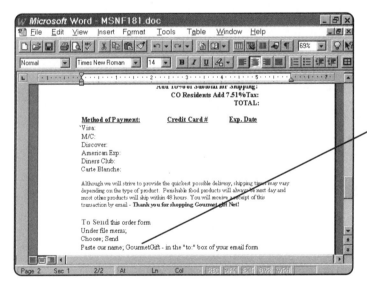

At the bottom of the form you'll see instructions on how to e-mail the order to the company once you've filled it in.

4. **Make a note** of the company's e-mail address.

5. Click on **File** in the menu bar. The File menu will appear.

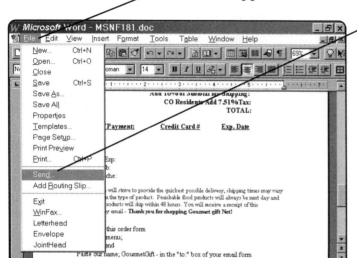

6. Click on **Send**. The Choose Profile dialog box will appear.

Note: Make sure the Profile Name box shows MS Exchange Settings. If it doesn't, click on the ▼ at the right of the box and select MS Exchange Settings from the pop-up menu.

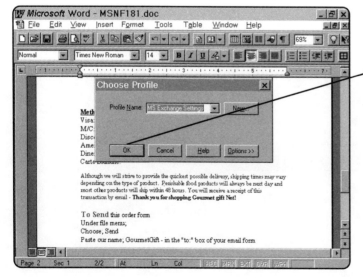

7. Click on **OK**. The New Message window will appear.

Notice that the order form has already been attached to this e-mail message and will be sent with the message.

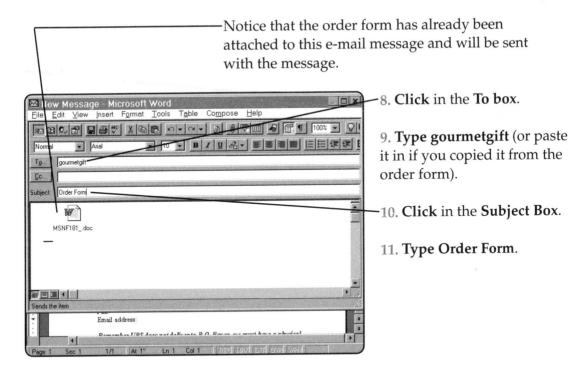

8. Click in the **To box**.

9. Type gourmetgift (or paste it in if you copied it from the order form).

10. Click in the **Subject Box**.

11. Type Order Form.

To actually send the order, you would now click on the Send icon in the toolbar near the top of the window. We'll skip this step for our example.

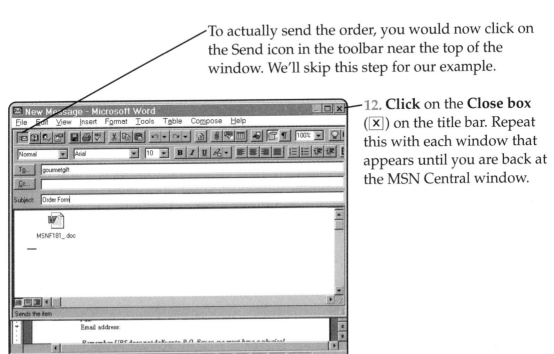

12. Click on the **Close box** (X) on the title bar. Repeat this with each window that appears until you are back at the MSN Central window.

Traveling through MSN

With so many travel options available these days, it helps to do your homework before heading out on a trip. The Microsoft Network has a variety of travel resources available to save you a visit to your local bookstore. You'll find them handy even if your trip doesn't take your any farther than your computer monitor! In this chapter, you will do the following:

✔ Browse through the Travel Forum
✔ Search for online travel guides
✔ Explore the Lanier Travel Guides
✔ Explore United Airlines' travel resources

BROWSING THE TRAVEL FORUM

In this section, you'll learn how to get to the Travel Forum. You'll also have a chance to take a look at one of the informative BBSs located in the Travel Forum.

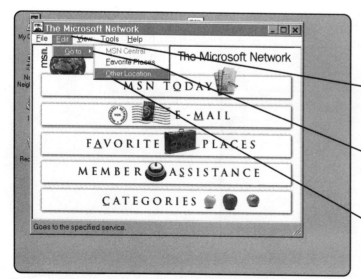

1. **Open The Microsoft Network** to **MSN Central**, if it isn't already on your screen.

2. **Click** on **Edit** in the menu bar. The Edit menu will appear.

3. **Move** the **mouse arrow** down to **Go to**. A second menu will appear.

4. **Click** on **Other Location**. The Go To Service dialog box will appear.

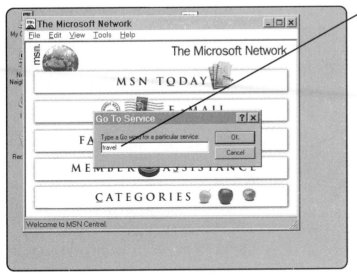

5. Type travel. (Travel is the Go Word for the Travel category.)

6. Press Enter on your keyboard (or click on OK). The Travel window will appear.

Note: The Travel category contains several interesting locations to explore. We'll come back to it later in this chapter to explore the United Airlines location. You may want to come back at the end of the chapter and explore some of the others on your own.

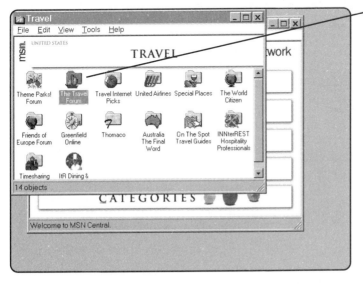

7. Click twice on the **The Travel Forum icon**. The Travel Forum window will appear.

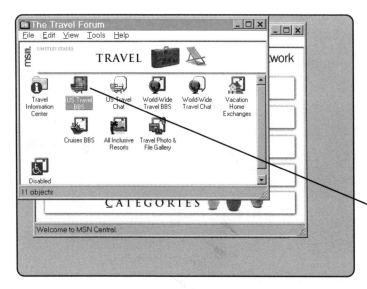

Looking Around a Travel BBS

The Travel Forum is made up primarily of BBSs, along with a few chat areas for travel-related chats. Let's take a look at one of the BBSs.

1. **Click twice** on the **US Travel BBS icon** (or any other BBS icon that interests you). The BBS window will appear.

All BBSs on The Microsoft Network work the same way, so refer back to Chapter 9 if you need a refresher on how to use them.

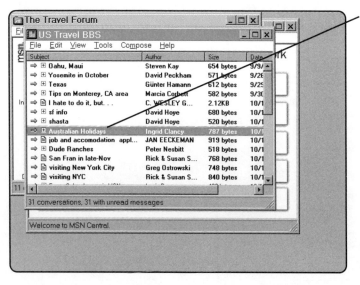

2. **Click twice** on a **message** that interests you. A message window will appear.

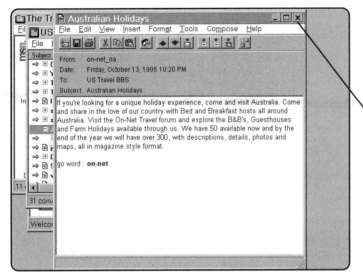

You can use the navigation tools in the toolbar to browse through the messages and conversations in the BBS.

3. When you're finished browsing, **click** on the **Close button** (🗙) on the title bar. The Travel Forum window will reappear.

SEARCHING FOR TRAVEL GUIDES

There are several travel guides available on the network. The best way to find them is to use Find.

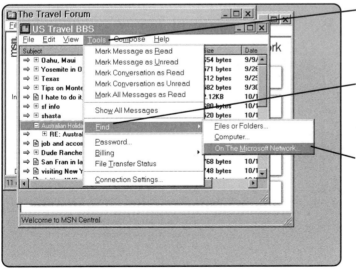

1. **Click** on **Tools** in the menu bar. The Tools menu will appear.

2. **Move** the **mouse arrow** down to **Find**. A second menu will appear.

3. **Click** on **On The Microsoft Network**. The Find window will appear.

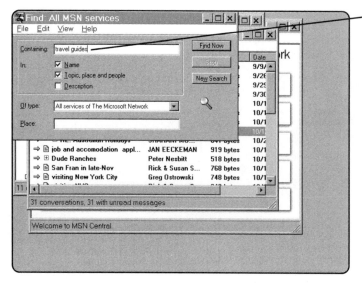

4. Type travel guides.

5. Press Enter on your keyboard (or click on Find Now). The Find window will expand and the network will begin its search. When it's finished, the results will be displayed in the bottom of the window.

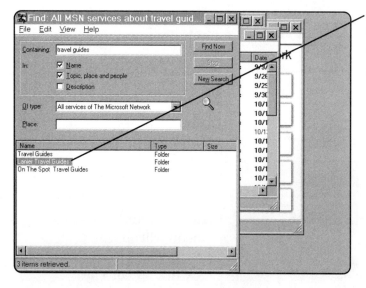

6. Click twice on **Lanier Travel Guides**. The Lanier Travel Guides window will appear.

EXPLORING
LANIER TRAVEL GUIDES

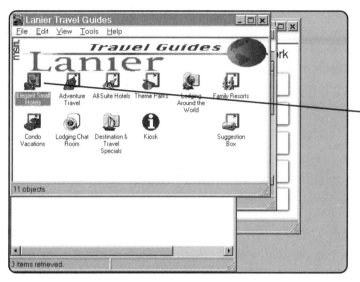

Lanier offers several useful travel guides to explore and each is set up in a BBS format.

1. Click twice on the **Elegant Small Hotels icon** (or any other BBS icon that interests you). The Elegant Small Hotels BBS window will appear. There are a lot of messages in this BBS, so there will be a small delay while the list is transferred.

Messages in this BBS begin with the name of the state in which the hotel is located. It's a lot easier to use if you sort the messages alphabetically.

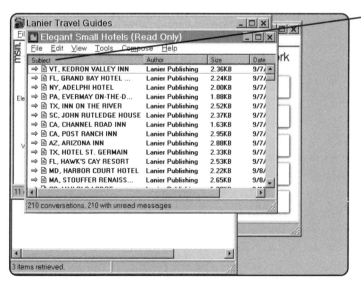

2. Click on the **Subject button** just above the message list. The list will be rearranged so that the messages appear in alphabetical order. (This is a shortcut to selecting "Arrange Messages by Subject" from the View menu, as we did in Chapter 9.)

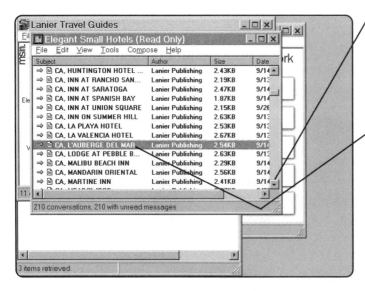

3. **Click repeatedly** on the ▼ at the bottom of the right scroll bar until the messages for the state you're interested in appear.

4. **Click twice** on the first message you would like to read. A message window will appear.

Notice that the phrase "Read-Only" appears in the title bar of this message and that the New Message and Reply to BBS buttons are grayed out in the toolbar. This indicates that the BBS is set up for viewing only, and you cannot post comments or respond to messages that appear in it.

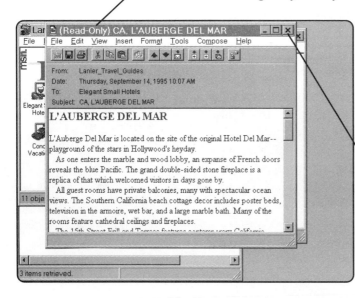

If you'd like to browse through this BBS, use the navigation tools in the toolbar to read the other messages.

5. When you're finished browsing, **click** on the **Close button** (⊠) on the title bar. Repeat this with each window that appears until you are back at the Travel category window.

FLYING BY UNITED AIRLINES

By the time you read this book, United Airlines should be offering a full online reservations system through The Microsoft Network. Unfortunately, this system was not available at the time we wrote this book, but we can show you how to get to United Airlines and show you one of the other neat resources they offer.

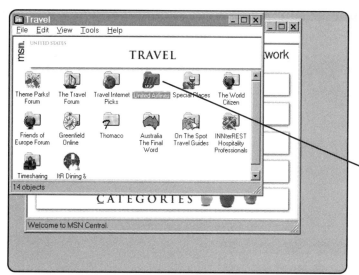

1. **Click twice** on the **United Airlines icon**. The United Airlines window will appear.

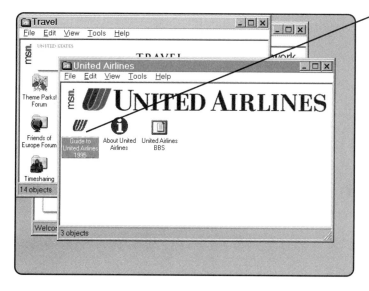

2. **Click twice** on the **Guide to United Airlines 1995 icon**. The United Airlines Guide window will appear.

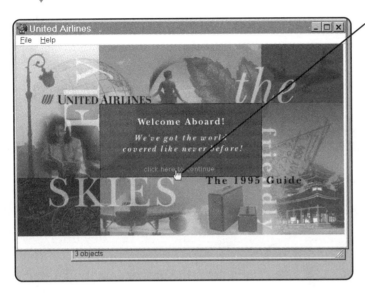

3. **Place** the **mouse arrow** over **Click here to continue**. The arrow will turn into a hand.

4. **Click** on **Click here to continue**. The window will display the Welcome to United Airlines 1995 Guide page.

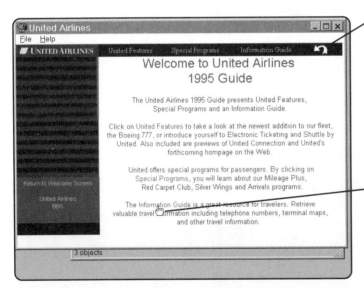

There are several resources to pick from on all of the United Airlines pages. You may want to come back later to explore some of them. To do so, click on the previous page icon near the top right of the window.

5. **Click** on **Information Guide**. The window will display the Welcome to the Information Guide page.

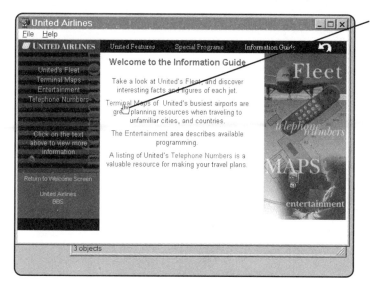

6. Click on **Terminal Maps**. The window will display the Terminal Maps page.

The Terminal Maps page opens to display a map of Chicago's O'Hare Airport. You can click on the name of a different airport in the list at the top right of the window if you'd like to see the map for that airport.

7. Click on the **Close button** (⊠) on the title bar. Repeat this with each window that appears until you are back at the MSN Central window.

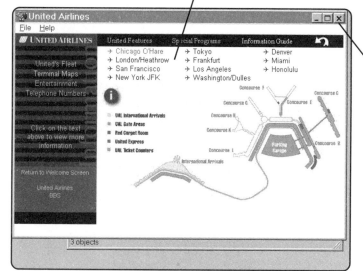

The Microsoft Network

Part V: Getting Computer Information and Software

Finding Technical Help

You can get a rich variety of online technical help for a number of hardware and software issues on The Microsoft Network. The type of online technical help available runs the gamut from tips to magazine articles and even training classes! In this chapter, you will do the following:

✔ Get online tips

✔ Go to the Microsoft Online Institute

✔ Browse through a list of online training classes

✔ Go to the online computer newsstand

✔ Download and print a magazine article

LOOKING FOR TIPS

The best place to go for online tips on Microsoft products is Cobb's PC Productivity Center.

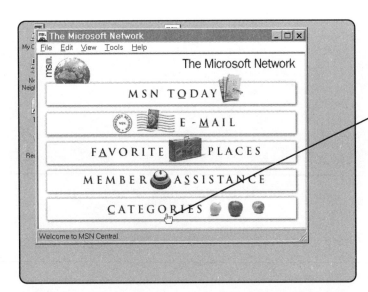

1. **Open The Microsoft Network** to **MSN Central,** if it isn't already on your screen.

2. **Place** the **mouse arrow** on **CATEGORIES.** The arrow will turn into a hand.

3. **Click** on **CATEGORIES.** The Categories window will appear.

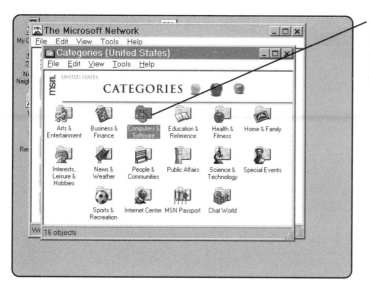

4. Click twice on the **Computers & Software icon.** The Computers & Software window will appear.

The Computers & Software category area is a great place to come for a wide variety of information on computers in general. We'll come back in the next chapter to look at the free (and almost free) software available here, but you may want to come back later and explore on your own.

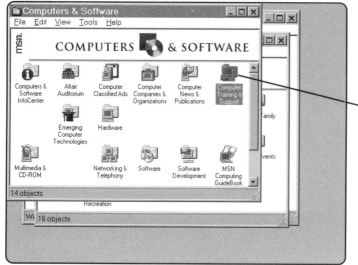

5. Click twice on the **Computer Training & Support icon.**

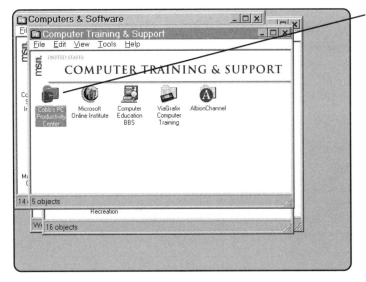

6. Click twice on the **Cobb's PC Productivity Center icon.** The Cobb's PC Productivity Center window will appear.

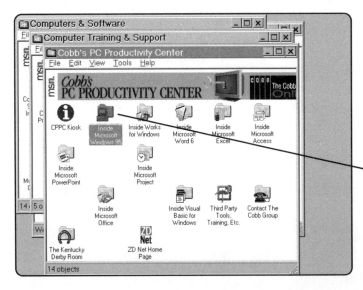

The Cobb Group publishes a number of excellent newsletters that are available by subscription through the mail. This area offers articles from those newsletters for downloading.

7. Click twice on the **Inside Microsoft Windows 95 icon.** The Inside Microsoft Windows 95 window will appear.

Checking the Rules

As you might guess by looking at the names of the icons, not everything in this window is free for the taking. The kiosk document explains the rules.

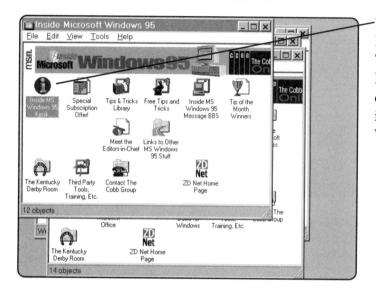

1. **Click twice** on the **Inside MS Windows 95 Kiosk icon**. The network will send the kiosk document to your computer and then open it with Microsoft Word or WordPad.

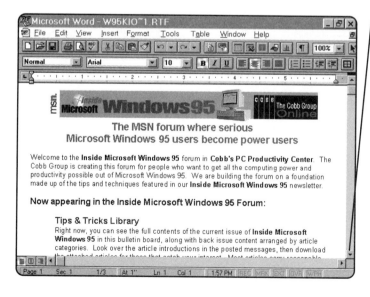

2. **Click repeatedly** on the ▼ at the bottom of the right scroll bar until the full text for the Tips & Tricks Library section comes into view.

As you can see, most of the articles in the Tips and Tricks Library BBS carry a surcharge of from $0.75 to $1.50, depending on the length of the article. The Free Tips & Tricks BBS, however, offers a free sampling of articles. We'll go there first.

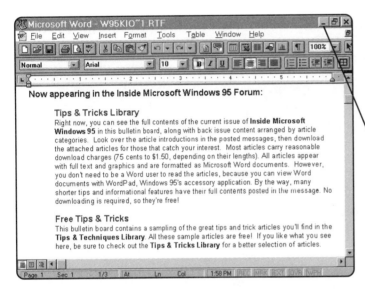

Note: You may want to print a copy of this document for future reference. To do so, click on Print in the File menu.

3. Click on the **Minimize button** (⬛) on the title bar. (We'll be downloading another document later, so there's no point in closing the program.) The Inside Microsoft Windows 95 window will reappear.

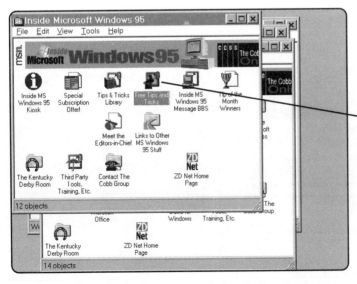

Looking at Tips

Let's see what kind of tips the Cobb Group has to offer.

1. Click twice on the **Free Tips and Tricks icon**. The Free Tips and Tricks BBS window will appear.

Notice that there are plain messages in this BBS (those with a 🗎 icon next to their names) as well as messages with attachments (those with a 📎 icon next to their names). Let's take a look at one of the messages with an attachment.

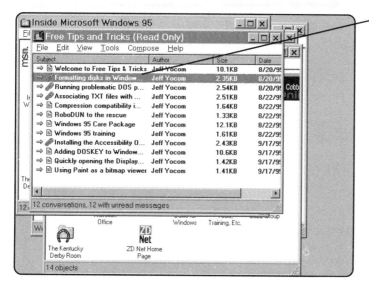

2. Click twice on **Formatting disks in Window** ... (or any other message name with an attachment). A message window will appear.

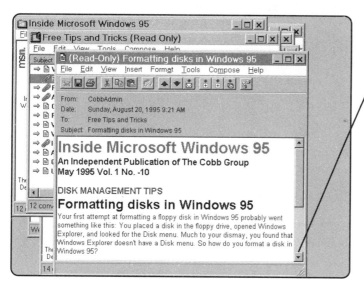

The message window will show you a brief description of the tip that is attached.

3. Click repeatedly on the ▼ at the bottom of the right scroll bar to scroll to the bottom of the message window.

At the end of the message you will see an icon for the attached document. Attached document icons can appear anywhere in a message, depending on where the person who created the message placed them. More than one document can be attached to a message.

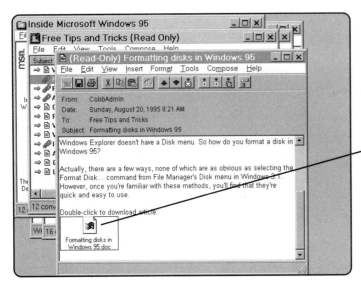

4. **Click twice** on the **attached document icon**. The Attached File Properties dialog box will appear.

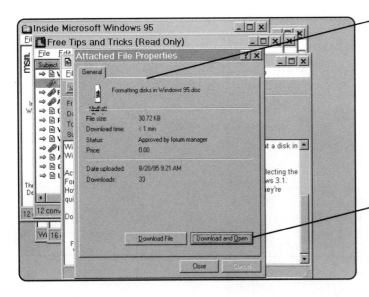

The Attached File Properties dialog box tells you how large the document is, how long it will take to download, and the price (if any). It also lets you know when it was uploaded and how many other people have downloaded it before you.

5. **Click** on the **Download and Open button**. The Downloading progress dialog box will appear.

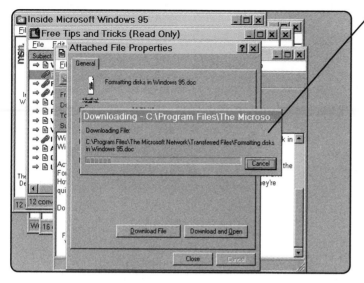

The Downloading progress dialog box lets you see how the file transfer is advancing as the network sends the file to your computer. If you change your mind about a download after you start it, you can end it at any time by clicking the Cancel button.

After the transfer is complete, the network will open the file using Microsoft Word or WordPad.

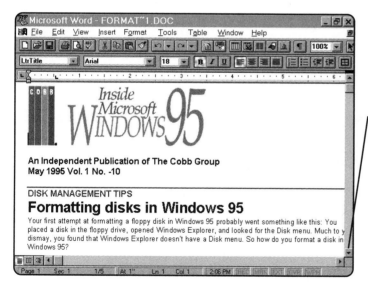

Notice that this tip is fully formatted. It also includes screen shots to help you follow along.

6. **Click repeatedly** on the ▼ at the bottom of the right scroll bar to see the screen shots in the tip.

You may want to print a copy of this tip before closing the program window. To do so, click on Print in the File menu.

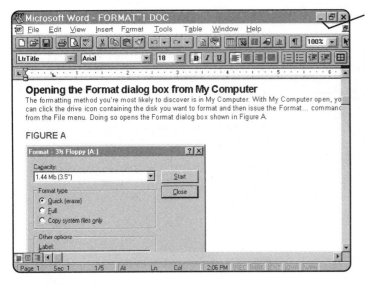

7. Click on the **Minimize button** ([_]) on the title bar. (We'll be using Word again later in the chapter.) The Inside Microsoft Windows window will reappear.

Browsing Other Tips

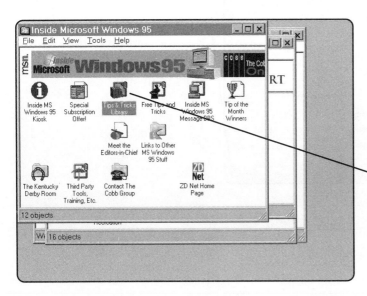

The other tips available carry a nominal charge for downloading, as you already know, but you can still look to see what's available. (Just think of it as Windows shopping!)

1. Click twice on the **Tips & Tricks Library icon**. The Tips & Tricks Library BBS window will appear.

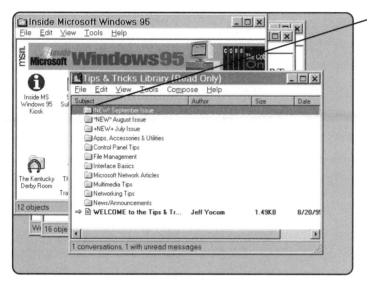

2. Click twice on a **folder icon** that looks interesting. (You will have more choices available than those shown here.) A BBS window will appear for that folder.

The plain messages are free to read. Those with attachments carry a surcharge, but you can open them by clicking twice on the tip name and read the message description for free. You will only be charged if you decide to download the attached document.

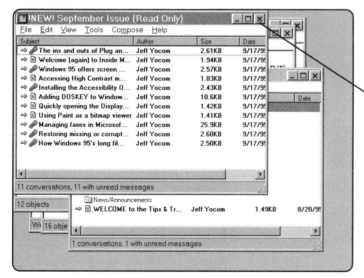

3. When you're done browsing, **click** on the **Close button** ($\boxed{\times}$) on the title bar. Repeat this with each window that appears until you are back at the Computer Training & Support window.

INVESTIGATING THE MICROSOFT ONLINE INSTITUTE

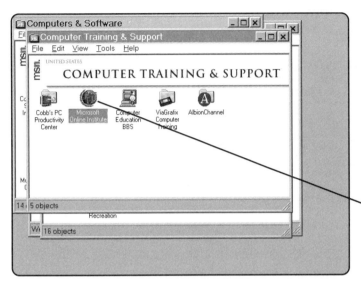

The Microsoft Online Institute offers a variety of online training classes from several different companies. Classes carry a fee, but they are a great way to get up to speed on the latest Microsoft software without having to leave your computer!

1. **Click twice** on the **Microsoft Online Institute icon**. The Microsoft Online Institute window will appear.

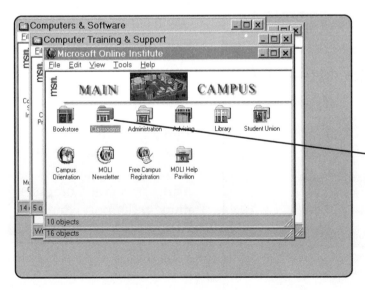

The Microsoft Online Institute offers several resources other than classes. You may want to come back later and explore the Bookstore and Library.

2. **Click twice** on the **Classrooms icon**. The Classrooms window will appear.

Getting an Orientation

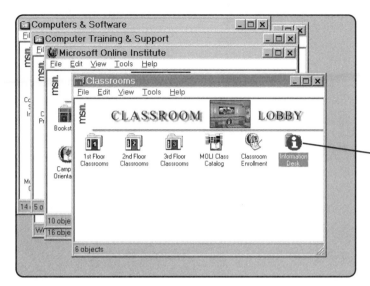

Whenever you enter a new area, it's always a good idea to check out the Information Desk or Kiosk for an overview of what's going on in the area.

1. Click twice on the **Information Desk icon**. The Information Desk window will appear.

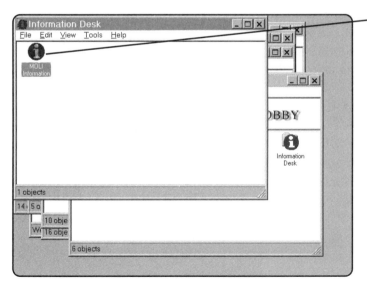

2. Click twice on the **MOLI Information icon**. The network will send the MOLI Information document to your computer and open it using Microsoft Word or WordPad.

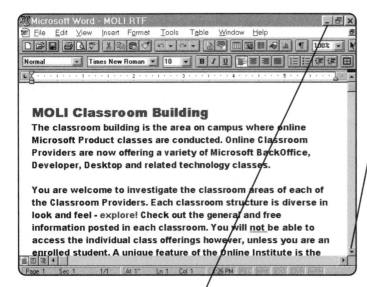

This document gives an overview of what the Microsoft Online Institute (or MOLI) classes are all about and explains a little about how they work.

3. **Click repeatedly** on the ▼ at the bottom of the right scroll bar to scroll through the document.

4. When you're done, **click** on the **Minimize button** (▬) on the title bar. The Classrooms window will reappear.

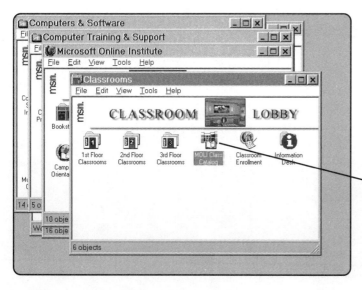

Checking the Class Catalog

Just like any institute of higher learning, MOLI has a class catalog to help you find the classes you need.

1. Click twice on the **MOLI Class Catalog icon**. The MOLI Class Catalog window will appear.

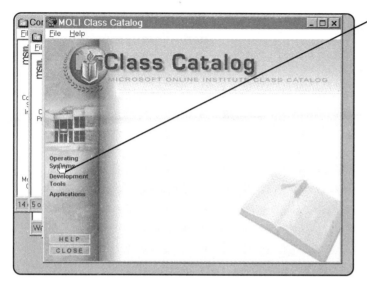

2. Click on **Operating Systems**. A list of operating systems will appear on the right side of the window.

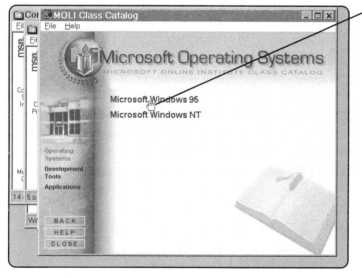

3. Click on **Windows 95**. A list of Windows 95 classes will appear on the right side of the window.

Courses are listed by the name of the company offering them.

4. Click repeatedly on the ▼ at the bottom of the right scroll bar to scroll through the list.

5. Click on the **name** of a company for a course that looks interesting. The course description will appear on the right side of the window.

The course description gives you all the relevant information about the content, cost, and location (within MOLI) of the course you selected.

Note: If you want to sign up for a course, click on the Enroll button and follow the directions.

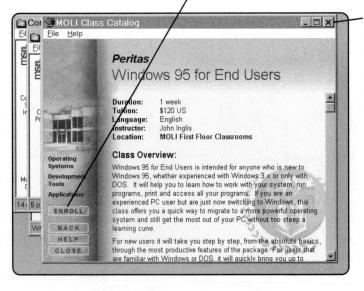

6. Click on the **Close button** (☒) on the title bar. Repeat this with each window that appears until you are back at the Computers & Software window.

CHECKING OUT MAGAZINES ONLINE

Another source for tips and technical information are online computer magazines.

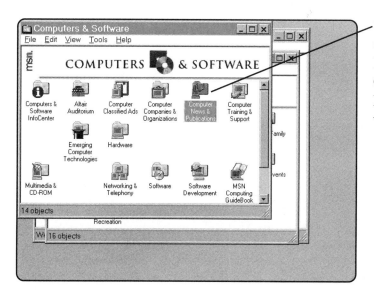

1. **Click twice** on the **Computer News & Publications icon**. The Computer News & Publications window will appear.

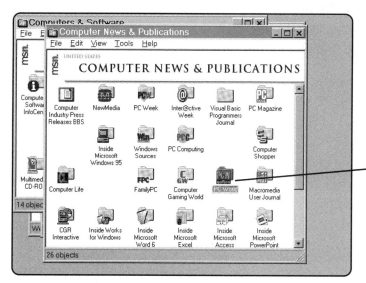

Note: Each of the online computer magazines is set up slightly differently and offers different resources. This is another good area to come back to and explore in more detail on your own.

2. **Click twice** on the **PC World icon**.

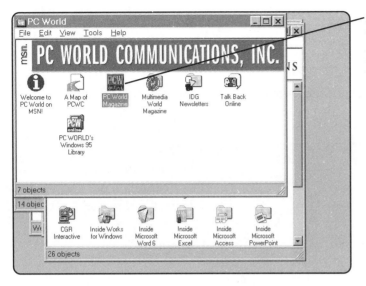

3. Click twice on the **PC World Magazine icon**. The PC World Online window will appear.

Note: Just like any regular newsstand magazine, online magazines come out with new issues on a regular basis. The contents and layout of the issue that appears on your screen will be different than the one shown here.

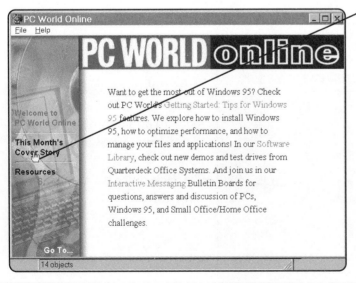

4. Click on **This Month's Cover Story**. A list of articles that accompany the cover story will appear on the right side of the screen.

Reading an Article

Once you decide on an article that interests you, reading it is easier than thumbing through a magazine!

1. **Click** on the **article name or icon**. A pop-up dialog box will appear with a brief description of the article.

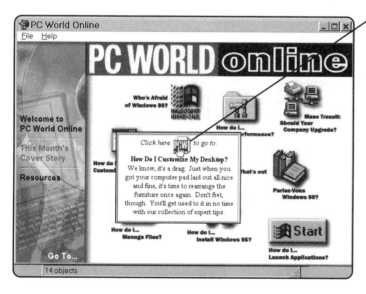

2. **Click** on the **icon** at the top of the pop-up dialog box. The network will send the article to your computer and then open it using Microsoft Word or WordPad.

Note: If you decide you don't want to read the article after seeing the description, click anywhere other than on the icon to close the pop-up dialog box.

If you want to read through the article, click repeatedly on the ▼ at the bottom of the right scroll bar.

If you want to print a copy of the article, click on Print in the File menu.

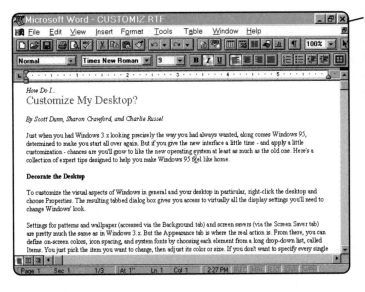

3. **Click** on the **Close button** (☒) on the title bar. Repeat this with each window that appears until you are back at the MSN Central window.

Adding to Your Software Collection

There's a time to work and a time to play, and right now it's play time! The Microsoft Network gives you access to one of the staples of human social life in the 90s: computer games. MSN has dozens of games that you can download (receive on your computer), and we'll show you how to find them. Kick back and get ready to have some fun. In this chapter, you will do the following:

✔ Find the Shareware Forum

✔ Download and install WinZip

✔ Find and download a shareware game

✔ Visit the Computer Games Forum

DISCOVERING SHAREWARE

Shareware is a nifty concept that allows you to download games and other programs from online services such as The Microsoft Network, try them out, and then pay a nominal amount if you decide to keep using them. MSN has a special section devoted to shareware.

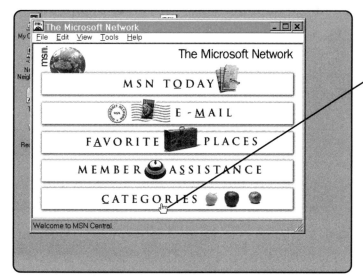

1. **Open The Microsoft Network** to **MSN Central**, if it isn't already on your screen.

2. **Place** the **mouse arrow** on **CATEGORIES**. The arrow will turn into a hand.

3. **Click** on **CATEGORIES**. The Categories window will appear.

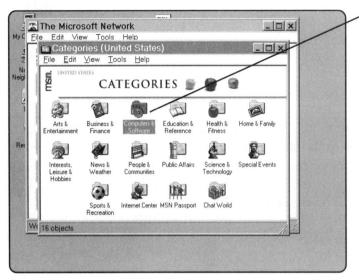

4. Click twice on the
Computers & Software icon.
The Computers & Software
window will appear.

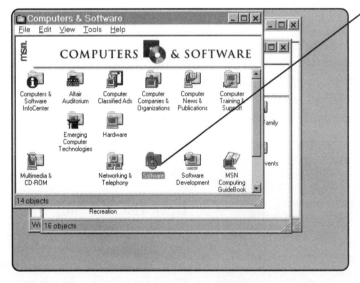

5. Click twice on the
Software icon. The Software
window will appear.

There is a tremendous variety of software available on The Microsoft Network for downloading to your computer. As you can see by the folders in this window, it's not just limited to games. Some of this software is free, while others carry a nominal fee only if you decide to keep and use the program. This is yet another area that you'll want to come back to later and explore on your own.

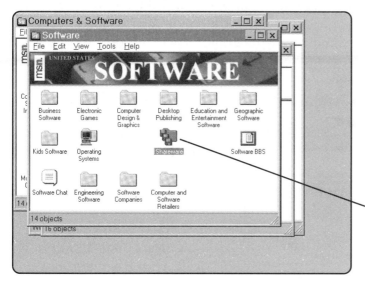

6. Click twice on the **Shareware icon**. The Shareware window will appear.

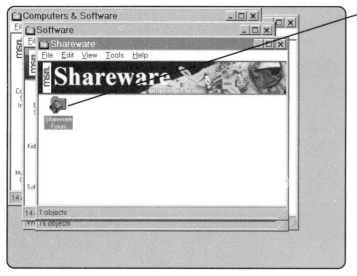

7. Click twice on the **Shareware Forum icon**. The Shareware Forum window will open.

DOWNLOADING WINZIP

The bigger a file, the more time it takes to download to your computer. Most online services therefore use a technique called *file compression* to keep file sizes as small as possible. Files are sent in compressed format, and you expand them to their original size on your computer using a special program. One such program is available as shareware, and is called WinZip.

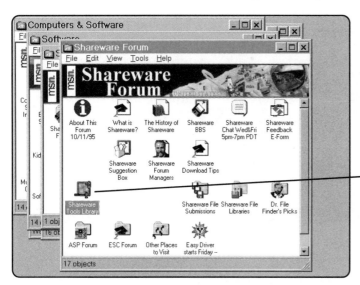

1. **Click twice** on the **Shareware Tools Library icon**. The Shareware Tools Library BBS window will appear.

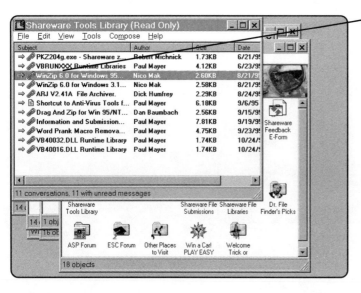

2. **Click twice** on **WinZip 6.0 for Windows 95**. A message window will appear.

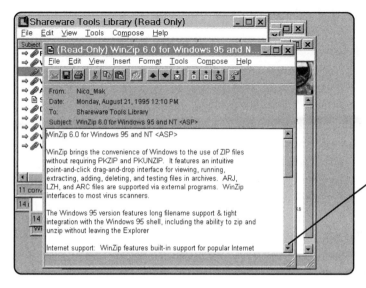

Note: The term ZIP refers to one particular method of compression (there are several). PKZIP and PKUNZIP are MS-DOS utilities that can be used to zip (compress) and unzip (expand) files.

3. Click repeatedly on the ▼ at the bottom of the right scroll bar to read through the message. Scroll all the way down to the bottom of the message.

Notice that the message includes information on the cost of the program, should you decide to keep and use it. Shareware registration is on the honor system, and we encourage you to register and support shareware authors. Information on how to register is usually provided with the program.

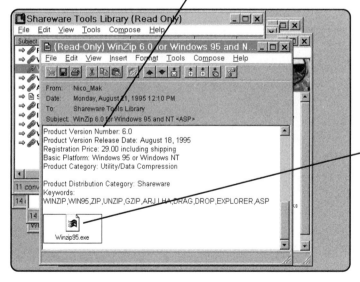

4. Click twice on the **Winzip95.exe icon**. The Attached File Properties dialog box will appear.

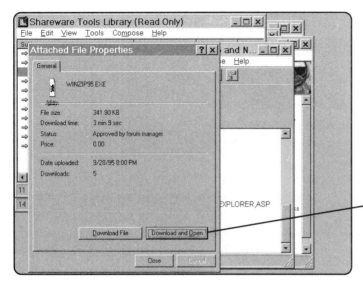

The Attached File Properties dialog box gives you a choice of simply downloading a file or downloading it and opening it. Since we'll need to use WinZip to expand any other files we download, we want to download and open it.

5. Click on **Download and Open**. A verification dialog box will open.

The verification dialog box lets you know how long it will take to download the file and makes sure you want to spend that much time downloading.

6. Click on **Yes**. The Downloading progress dialog box will appear.

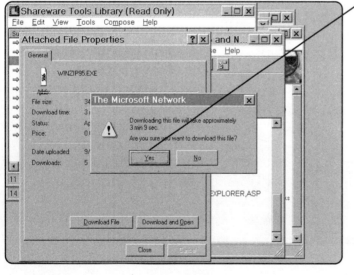

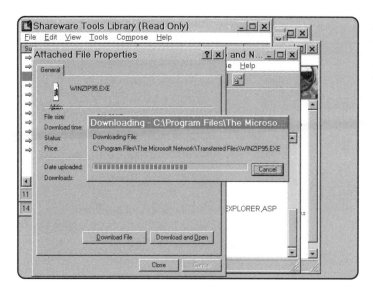

After the transfer is complete, the network will open the file and the WinZip Self-Extractor window will appear.

INSTALLING WINZIP

Installing WinZip is a relatively painless procedure that requires very little thought on your part!

Note: Click in the Unzip To box and type the name of another directory if you don't want to use the one shown here. After WinZip is set up and you no longer need them, you will probably want to find and delete the setup files.

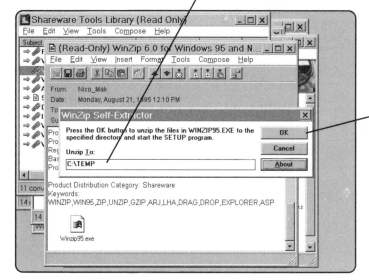

1. **Click** on **OK**. The file will expand itself, and then the WinZip Setup window will appear.

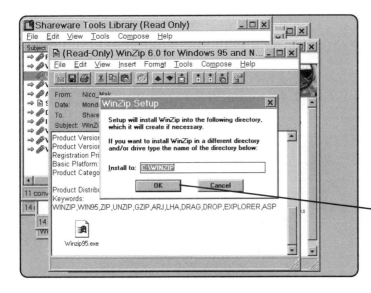

Note: If you prefer to install WinZip in a directory other than the one shown in this window, you can type a different directory name. This will be the directory where the working files for WinZip will remain as long as you keep the program.

2. Click on **OK**. The Welcome to WinZip dialog box will appear.

Note: Make sure there is a dot in the circle before Express Setup as shown here. If not, click on Express Setup to put one there.

3. Click on **OK**. The License Agreement and Warranty Disclaimer dialog box will appear.

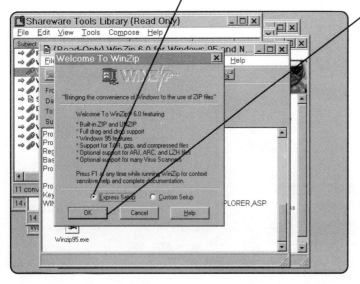

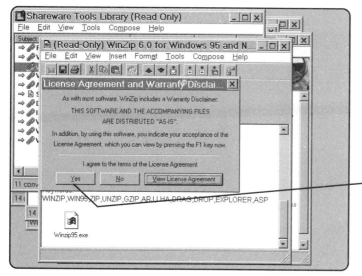

Note: You should press the F1 key on your keyboard or click on View License Agreement now and read this. It gives you important legal information on how you are allowed to use the software.

4. Click on **Yes**. The software will be installed. Next, the program window will open and a WinZip information dialog box will appear.

This dialog box lets you know that a tutorial is available from the program's Help menu. You can press F1 to view the tutorial now, but since you're still online, you'll probably want to look at it later.

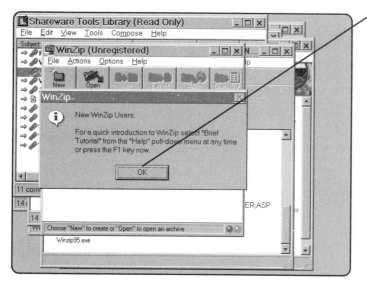

5. Click on **OK**. The WinZip program window will appear.

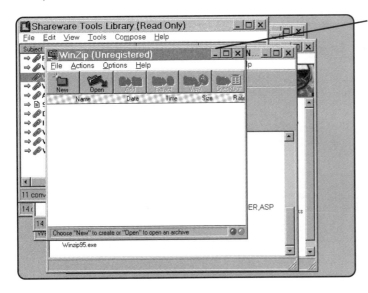

6. **Click** on the **Minimize button** (☐) on the title bar. (You'll be downloading and expanding another file in a moment, so there's no point in closing the program window.) The WinZip Program Manager window will appear.

As you can see, the installation process created a program manager window for WinZip. It contains the program, an uninstall program in case you decide to remove WinZip from you computer, the online manual (which is opened automatically when you use WinZip's Help menu), and a README file. You may want to open the README file on you own. It contains information about the program and how to register your copy.

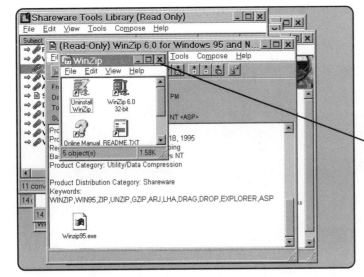

7. **Click** on the **Close button** (☒) on the WinZip title bar. Repeat this with each window that appears until you are back at the Shareware Forum window.

FINDING A GAME

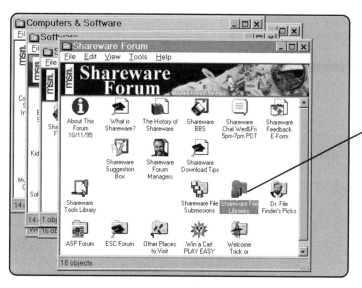

There are several places on The Microsoft Network to find game programs to download. We'll show you two of them in this chapter.

1. Click twice on the **Shareware File Libraries icon**. The Shareware File Libraries window will appear.

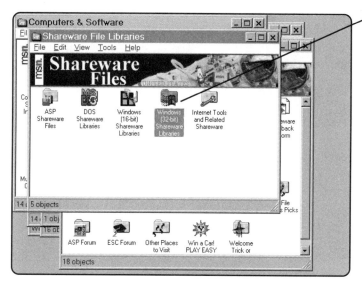

2. Click twice on the **Windows (32-bit) Shareware Libraries icon**. The Windows (32-bit) Shareware Libraries window will appear.

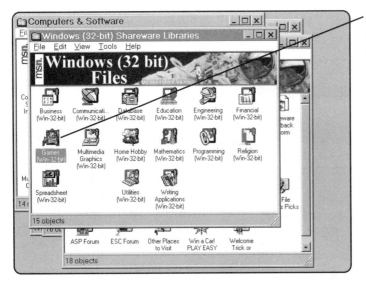

3. Click twice on the **Games (Win-32-bit) icon**. The Games (Win-32-bit) BBS window will appear.

4. Click twice on the **name** of a game that looks interesting. A message window will appear.

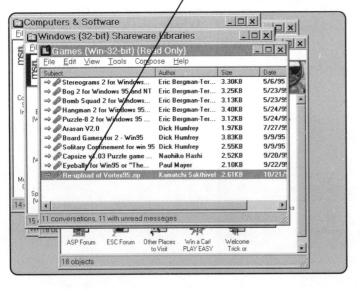

Note: The number of shareware files available from The Microsoft Network grows on a daily basis. The list you see will be different than the one shown here.

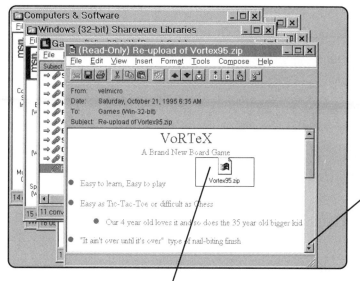

Downloading a Game

The process of downloading a game program is the same as the process for downloading WinZip or any other attached file you might come across.

1. If necessary, **click repeatedly** on the ▼ at the bottom of the right scroll bar until you come to the icon for the attached file.

2. **Click twice** on the **attached file icon** (in this example, it's Vortex95.zip). The Attached File Properties dialog box will appear.

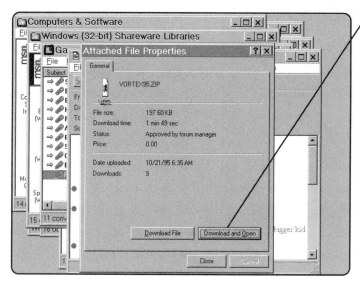

3. **Click** on **Download and Open**. A Microsoft Network dialog box will appear.

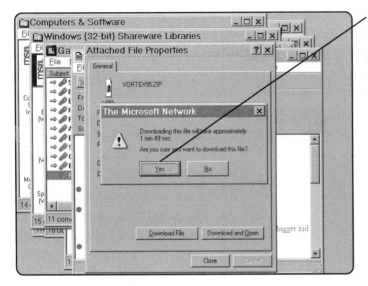

4. Click on **Yes**. The Downloading progress dialog box will appear. When the download is complete, WinZip will open the file.

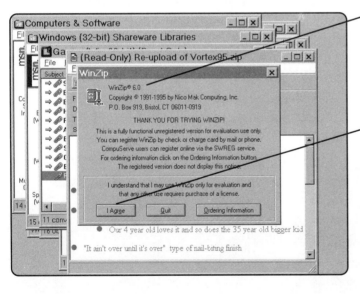

Note: As long as you are using an unregistered copy of WinZip, every time you run the program this reminder window will appear.

5. Click on **I Agree**. The WinZip program window will appear.

Expanding the File

The WinZip window shows all the files that have been compressed together into the file you down-loaded. We want to extract and expand these files.

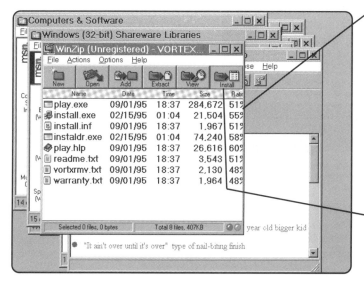

Notice that this window also shows how much smaller the compressed files are relative to the expanded versions. As you can see, most of these compressed files are roughly half the size of the originals. This means they take only half as much time to download.

1. Click on the **Install button** at the top right of the window. The Install dialog box will appear.

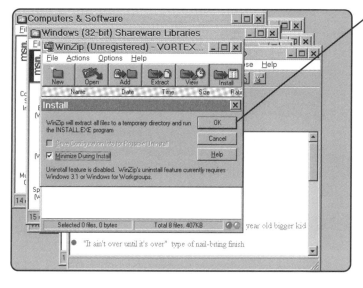

2. Click on **OK**. WinZip will expand the program files and run the install program.

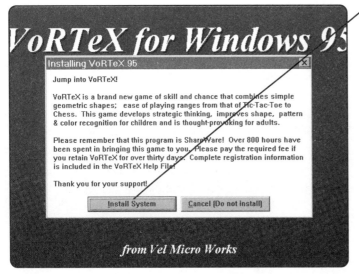

3. Click on **Install System**. The program will be installed on your computer. When it is finished, a confirmation dialog box will appear.

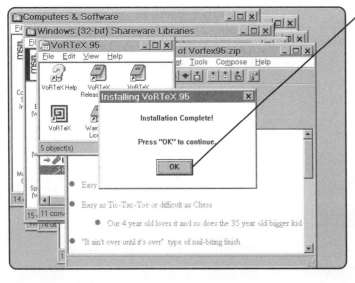

4. Click on **OK**. The Vortex Program Manager window will appear.

At this point, you can try the game out if you like by clicking twice on the game icon. (But remember, you're still online!) When you're done, close the program window.

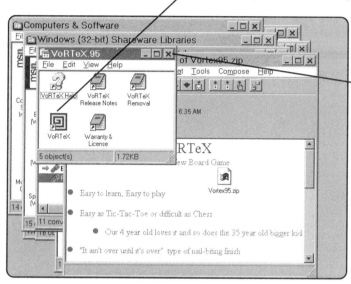

5. Click on the **Close button** ([X]) on the title bar. Repeat this with each window that appears until you are back at the Software window.

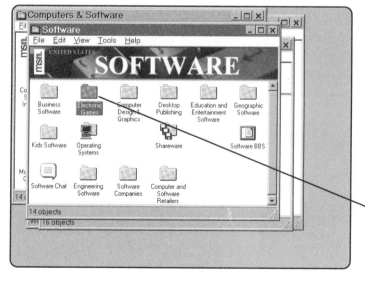

FINDING OTHER GAMES

As mentioned earlier, there are several places on The Microsoft Network where games can be found. The Electronic Games forum is one of them!

1. Click twice on the **Electronic Games icon**. The Electronic Games window will appear.

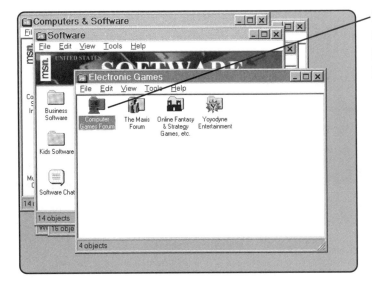

2. Click twice on the **Computer Games Forum icon**. The Computer Games Forum window will appear.

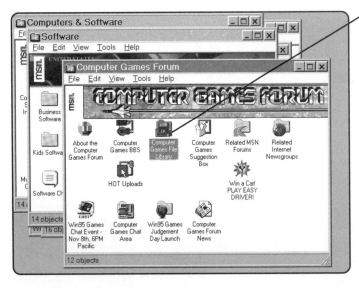

3. Click twice on the **Computer Games File Library icon**. The Computer Games File Library window will appear.

Each of the folders shown in this window is a BBS full of game programs, support files, and demos of popular games. You have all the skills necessary to open these BBSs, read the file descriptions, and download the files that interest you. We'll leave it up to you to explore them on your own.

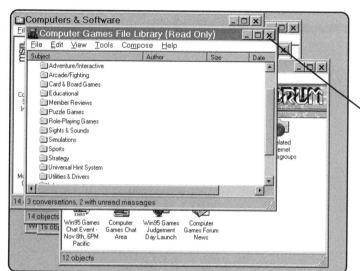

4. When you're done browsing, **click** on the **Close button** ([X]) on the title bar. Repeat this with each window that appears until you are back at the MSN Central window.

The Microsoft Network

Part VI: Using MSN Resources

Keeping Up with Current Events

Too much time online may cause you to loose track of what's going on in the world around you, so it's a good thing that The Microsoft Network offers a full range of news services! You can find all the latest headlines, sports, and even weather forecasts online with just a few clicks of your mouse. In this chapter, you will do the following:

✔ Explore MSN News

✔ Check your local weather forecast

✔ Discover MSN's other news resources

EXPLORING MSN NEWS

In this section, you'll get right into the day's top headlines and find out how to use MSN's NewsView program to skim through the stories that interest you.

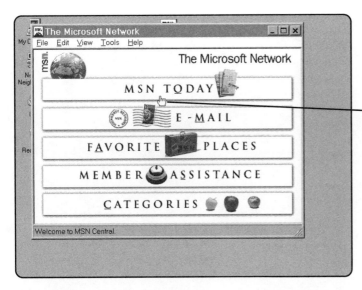

1. **Open The Microsoft Network** to **MSN Central**, if it isn't already on your screen.

2. **Place** the **mouse arrow** on **MSN TODAY**. The arrow will turn into a hand.

3. **Click** on **MSN TODAY**. The MSN Today window will appear.

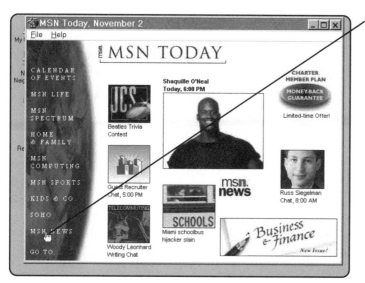

4. Click on **MSN NEWS.** The MSN News window will appear.

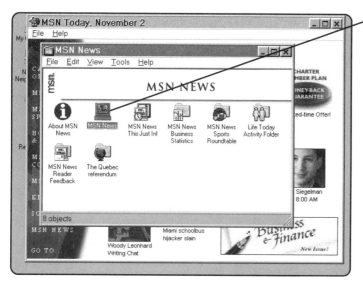

5. Click twice on the **MSN News icon**. A downloading progress window will appear.

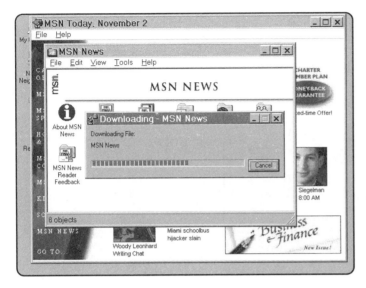

Note: MSN News uses a special program called NewsView to display the news. The first time you open MSN News the network will send this program and several associated files to your computer. This may take a couple of minutes, so don't panic! Each time you open MSN News after that, the network will just send a file with the current news stories to your computer.

After the download is complete, the MSN News window will appear with the MSN News front page.

Reading the News

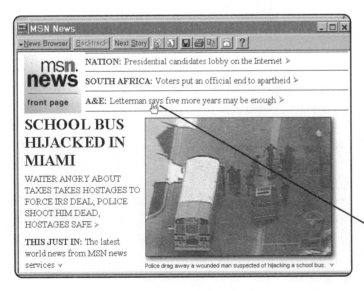

The front page shows a list of the major headlines for this issue of MSN News.

Note: The news changes daily (we hope), so the headlines and articles you see on your screen will not be the same as the ones shown in this chapter.

1. **Click** on a **headline** that interests you. The story for that headline will appear.

Notice that this particular article is part of the Arts & Entertainment section of MSN News, as you can see from the top right corner of the window. MSN News has several sections just like a regular newspaper. You'll see in a moment how to go to a specific section.

Many stories include links to other areas of MSN that are related to the story, such as the one shown here.

2. **Click repeatedly** on the ▼ at the bottom of the right scroll bar to scroll through the story. Stop when you come to a link.

Note: If you scroll down far enough, you'll see that each section contains more than one story.

3. **Click** on the **link**. A pop-up dialog box will appear.

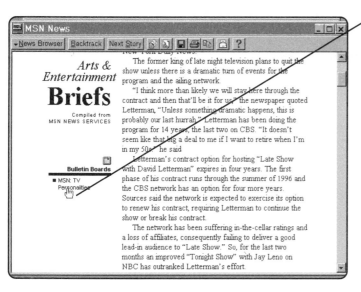

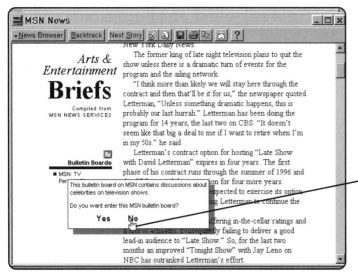

The pop-up dialog box gives you a description of the linked area and asks you whether or not you want to enter that area. If you click on Yes, a window will open for that area. We'll skip doing this for our example.

4. Click on **No**. The dialog box will disappear.

Jumping Between Sections

As mentioned earlier, MSN News is laid out just like a newspaper, with different sections on different news topics. You can quickly jump from section to section using the News Browser menu.

1. Click on the **News Browser button** in the toolbar at the top of the window. The News Browser menu will appear.

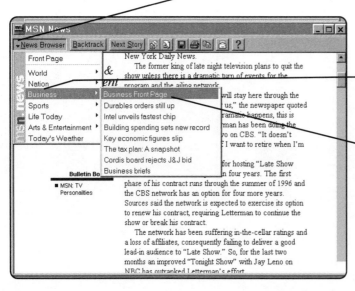

2. Move the **mouse arrow** down to **Business**. A second menu will appear.

3. Click on **Business Front Page**. The front page of the business section will appear.

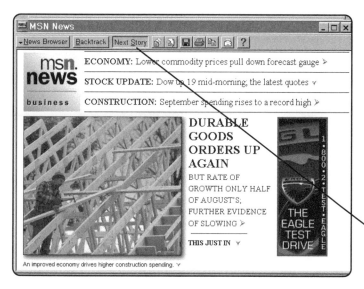

Notice that the front page of each section is set up just like the front page of MSN News, with a list of headlines for the top stories in the section.

If you want to read all the stories in a section, you can do so by using the Next Story button.

4. Click on the **Next Story button** in the toolbar. The next story will appear.

Backtracking

There are two ways to backtrack through MSN News stories that you have already read. The most obvious way is by clicking on the Backtrack button in the toolbar. This will take you back one story each time you click it. We'll let you try this on your own. The other way is by using the List of Previously Read Stories button.

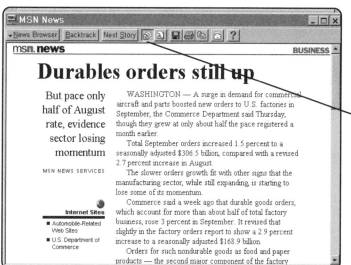

1. Click on the **List of Previously Read Stories button** in the toolbar. The History dialog box will appear.

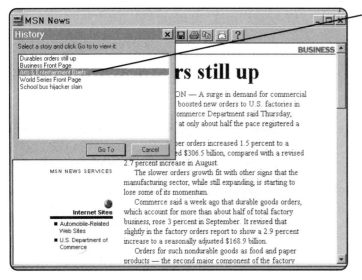

2. Click twice on the **name** of the page you want to go back to. The page will appear in the MSN News window behind the History dialog box.

The History window remains on the screen after the page appears; presumably, so you can make sure it's really the page you want.

3. Click on the **Close button** (⊠) on the title bar of the History dialog box. The dialog box will disappear.

Searching for News

You may only be interested in articles about a particular subject, person, or company. MSN News offers a way to search the news for exactly what you're looking for.

1. **Click** on the **Search News for Specific Topic button** in the toolbar at the top of the window. The Find MSN News Article dialog box will appear.

2. **Type** the **topic or name** you're interested in.

3. **Press Enter** on your keyboard (or click on Find Now). The network will begin its search. When it's finished, the results will be displayed in the lower part of the dialog box.

4. **Click twice** on the **name** of the article you want to read. The article will appear in the MSN News window behind the Find MSN News Article dialog box.

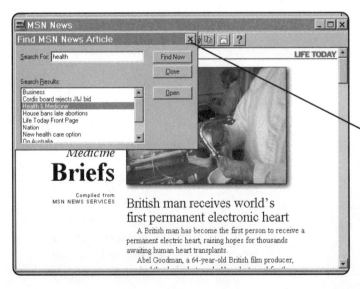

The Find MSN News Article window will stay visible so that you can check the article and make sure it's the one you want.

5. **Click** on the **Close button** (☒) on the Find MSN News Article title bar. The Find MSN News Article dialog box will disappear.

CHECKING THE WEATHER

Online weather forecasts are one of the greatest features of the computer age. Never again will you be forced to sit through the nightly news just to find out if you can have an outdoor party this weekend!

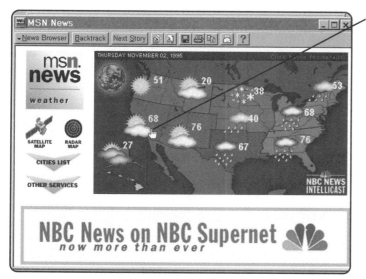

1. **Click** on the **News Browser button** in the toolbar at the top of the window. The News Browser menu will appear.

2. **Click** on **Today's Weather**. The weather page will appear.

3. **Click** on the **region** you would like more detail for. The NBC News Intellicast window will appear with a more detailed map.

Getting a City Forecast

You can get a forecast for the major cities in your region.

1. **Click** on **city view**. A pop-up window will appear.

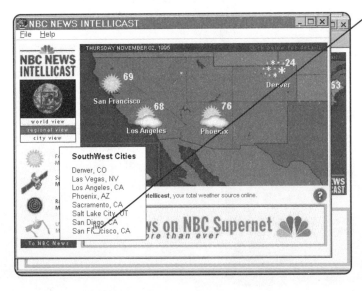

2. **Click** on the **city** you would like a forecast for. A weather window for that city will appear.

The city weather window provides a four-day outlook for the city you selected. You can also get more detail on the forecast.

3. **Click** on **Click here for more detail on the forecast**. A pop-up window will appear.

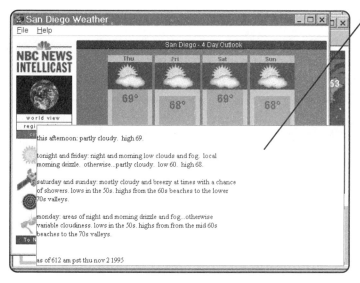

4. When you're done with the forecast, **click anywhere** in the window. The pop-up window will disappear.

Notice that there are other features to explore in the weather window, including a satellite map and a radar map. We'll leave these for you to explore on your own.

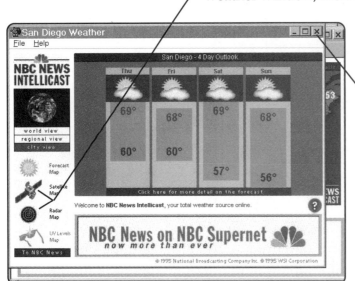

5. Click on the **Close button** ([X]) on the title bar. Repeat this with each window that appears until you are back at the MSN Central window.

LOCATING OTHER NEWS SERVICES

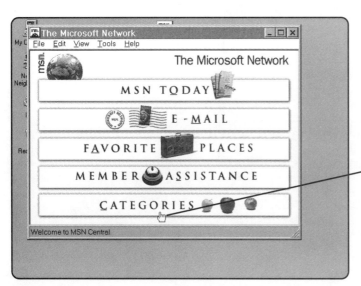

There are several other news services on The Microsoft Network, including NBC News. We don't have enough space to explore them all here, but we can show you how to find them.

1. Click on **CATEGORIES**. The Categories window will appear.

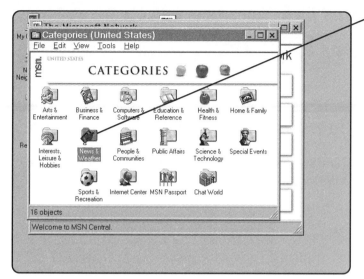

2. **Click twice** on the **News & Weather icon**. The News & Weather window will appear.

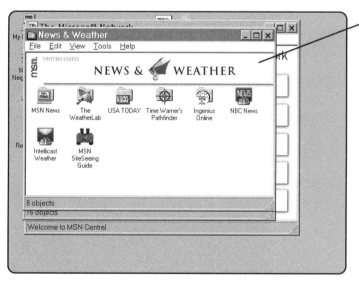

There's a lot to explore in this window, so we'll leave you to it.

Finding Business and Financial Information

If your interest in The Microsoft Network is more business-related, you'll be glad to know that there are plenty of business and financial resources available. These resources will help you do everything from managing your portfolio to operating a home office. In this chapter, you will do the following:

✔ Learn how to navigate the Business & Finance Category

✔ Get investment tips from Max's Investment World

✔ Download and print a company profile from Hoover's Business Resources

✔ Locate the Business & Finance GuideBook

LOCATING BUSINESS RESOURCES

In this section, you will learn how to navigate the Business & Finance category using a special MSN resource.

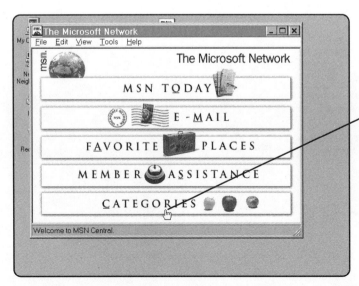

1. **Open The Microsoft Network** to **MSN Central**, if it isn't already on your screen.

2. **Place** the **mouse arrow** on **CATEGORIES**. The arrow will turn into a hand.

3. **Click** on **CATEGORIES**. The Categories window will appear.

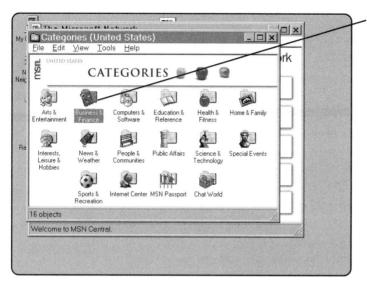

4. Click twice on the **Business & Finance icon**. The Business & Finance window will appear.

You may remember this category from Chapter 9, when you explored BBSs in the Investing area. As you can see, there are quite a few other resources available to explore. Fortunately, all are easily accessible from one place.

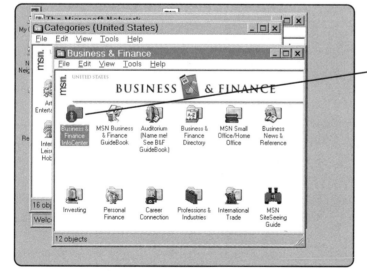

5. Click twice on the **Business & Finance Info-Center icon**. The Business & Finance InfoCenter window will appear.

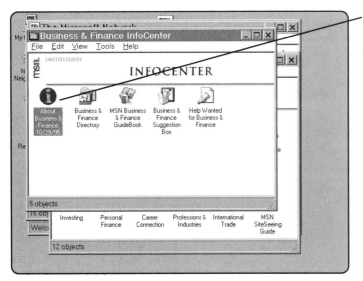

6. Click twice on the **About Business & Finance icon**. The network will send About Business & Finance Category to your computer, then open it.

Using the About Business & Finance Category Guide

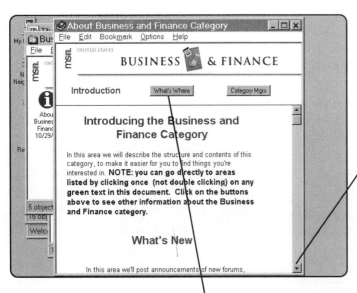

About Business & Finance Category is a resource that offers an overview of the Business & Finance Category, and helps you navigate quickly to different business and finance areas.

If you want to read the overview, click repeatedly on the ▼ at the bottom of the right scroll bar to scroll through the rest of the text.

1. Click on the **What's Where button** near the top of the window. The What's Where in Business & Finance page will appear.

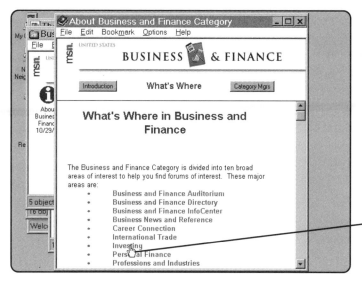

The What's Where in Business and Finance page begins by dividing the category into general areas of interest. You can select from these areas to see what resources are available for each. As an example, we'll take a look at the investing resources.

2. Click on **Investing**. The page will jump to the Investing section.

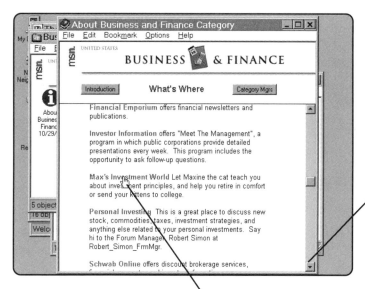

GETTING AN INVESTMENT TIP

Each resource listing includes a description of the resource. You can browse through these descriptions to find a resource that interests you.

1. Click repeatedly on the ▼ at the bottom of the right scroll bar until **Max's Investment World** appears.

2. Click on **Max's Investment World**. The Max's Investment World window will appear.

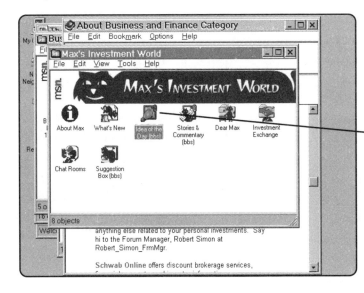

There are several places to explore in this forum. We'll look at one and let you explore the others on your own.

3. Click twice on the **Idea of the Day (bbs) icon**. The Idea of the Day BBS window will appear. (See Chapter 9 for details on using BBSs.)

Notice that these messages have 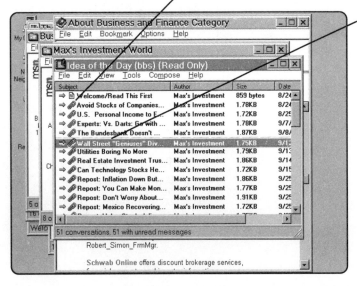 icons next to them, indicating that each has an attached document.

4. Click twice on a **message topic** that interests you. A message window will open.

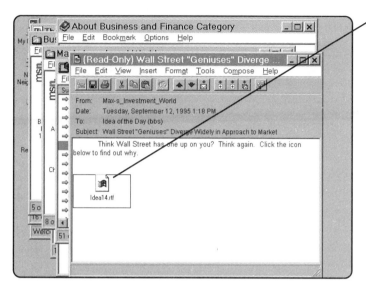

5. Click twice on the **attached document icon**. The Attached File Properties dialog box will appear.

Note: This document, along with many others in the Business & Finance category, carries a fee for downloading. The Attached File Properties dialog box alerts you to the amount of this fee, as does a warning dialog box that appears before the download starts. If you download the file, the fee will be charged to your MSN account.

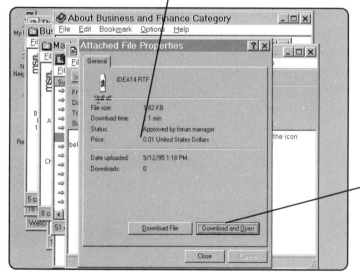

6. If you don't mind paying the fee, **click** on **Download and Open**. A warning dialog box will appear.

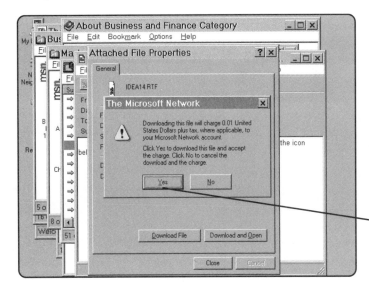

The network is very nice about making sure that you don't accidentally download a file that carries a charge without realizing it. This warning dialog box will appear whenever you begin such a download to make sure that you accept the charge.

7. **Click** on **Yes**. The network will send the file to your computer and open it using Microsoft Word or WordPad.

8. **Click repeatedly** on the ▼ at the bottom of the right scroll bar to read through the document.

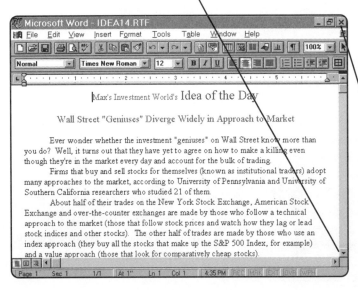

If you want to print the document, click on Print in the File menu.

9. **Click** the **Close button** (☒) on the title bar. Repeat this with each window that appears until you are back at the About Business and Finance Category window.

PRINTING A COMPANY PROFILE

Another handy resource in the Business & Finance category is the Hoover's Business Resources forum, which includes complete profiles of a number of different companies. In this section, you'll learn how to download and print one of these profiles.

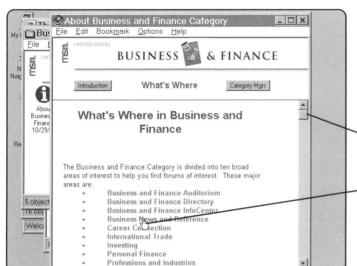

1. Drag the **scroll box** to the top of the scroll bar.

2. Click on **Business News and Reference**. The page will jump to the Business News and Reference section.

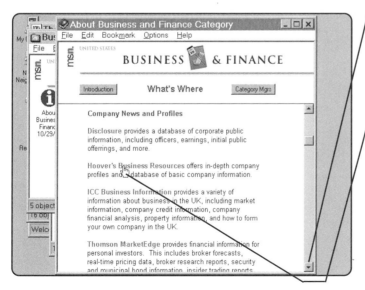

3. Click repeatedly on the ▼ at the bottom of the right scroll bar until you see **Hoover's Business Resources**.

4. Click on **Hoover's Business Resources**. The Hoover's Business Resources window will appear.

Downloading a Profile

For our example, we'll be downloading a profile from the In-Depth Company Profiles BBS. These profiles carry a charge of $1.00 each. If you prefer not to pay this charge, there are several free profiles available in the Free Candy Company Profiles BBS that is also shown in this window. These profiles are stored as BBS messages rather than attached files.

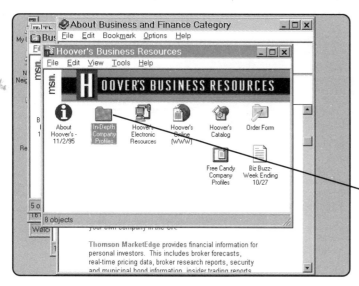

1. **Click twice** on the **In-Depth Company Profiles icon**. The In-Depth Company Profiles window will appear.

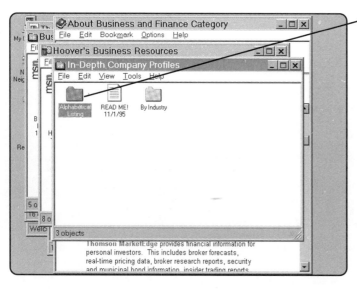

2. **Click twice** on the **Alphabetical Listing icon**. The Alphabetical Listing window will appear.

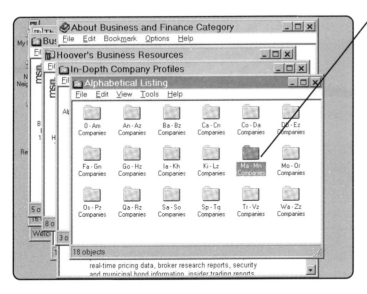

3. **Click twice** on a **Folder icon**. The window for that folder will appear.

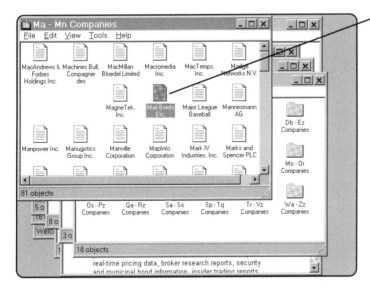

4. **Click twice** on the **document icon** for a company that interests you. A warning dialog box will appear.

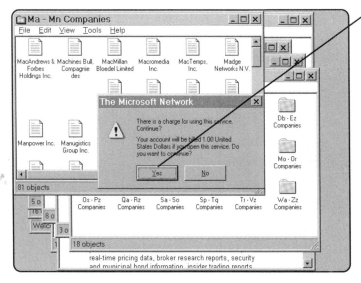

5. **Click** on **Yes** to approve the $1.00 charge for this document. The network will send the document to your computer and open it using Microsoft Word or WordPad. The $1.00 fee will be charged to your MSN account.

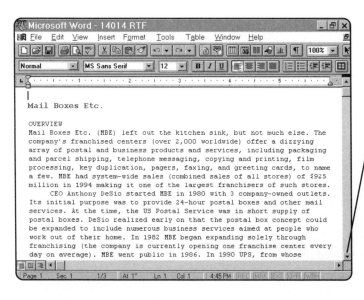

Each profile includes a variety of information about the company you selected, including an overview, key competitors, and financial information.

6. **Click repeatedly** on the ▼ at the bottom of the right scroll bar to scroll through the rest of the profile.

Printing a Profile

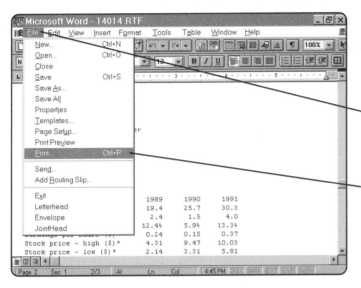

You'll probably want to print a copy of any profiles you download for future reference.

1. Click on **File** in the menu bar. The File menu will appear.

2. Click on **Print**. The Print dialog box will appear.

3. Click on **OK**. The profile will be sent to your printer.

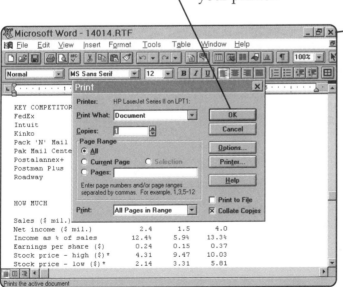

4. Click on the **Close box** ([X]) on the title bar. Repeat this with each window that appears until you are back at the Business & Finance category window.

FINDING THE MSN BUSINESS & FINANCE GUIDEBOOK

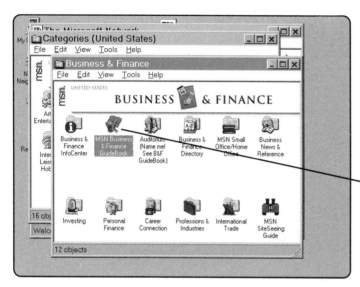

There is one last resource you should take a look at that deals with business and finance: the MSN Business & Finance GuideBook. We don't have space to explore it here, but we will show you how to get to it.

1. **Click twice** on the **MSN Business & Finance GuideBook icon**. The MSN Business & Finance Guide-Book window will appear.

The Business & Finance GuideBook works just like other MSN GuideBooks. See Chapter 6 for details.

Using the Encyclopedia and Research Tools

MSN's online version of Encarta is a slimmed-down version of Microsoft's best-selling CD-ROM encyclopedia (only the video and audio clips are missing). You'll find this terrific resource to be invaluable for a school paper or research project. In addition, the rich variety of MSN's online forums can supplement almost any topic. In this chapter, you will use these resources to do the following:

✔ Use Encarta to look up information
✔ Search MSN forums

SETTING UP ENCARTA

In this section, you will find and install the online version of Encarta, and then use it to research a topic.

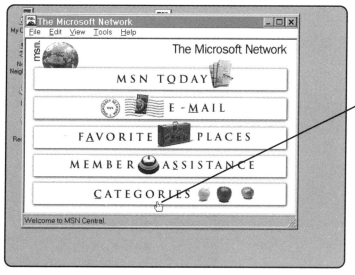

1. Open The Microsoft Network to **MSN Central**, if it isn't already on your screen.

2. Place the **mouse arrow** on **CATEGORIES**. The arrow will turn into a hand.

3. Click on **CATEGORIES**. The Categories window will appear.

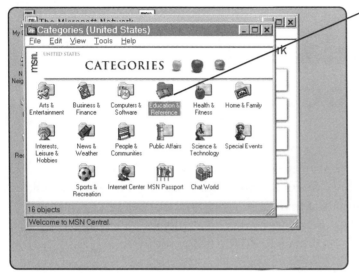

4. **Click twice** on the **Education & Reference icon**. The Education & Reference window will appear.

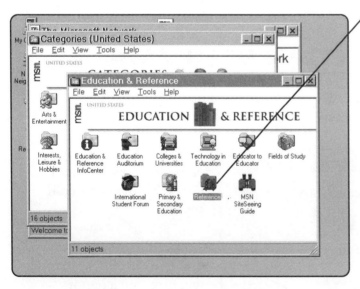

5. **Click twice** on the **Reference icon**. The Reference window will appear.

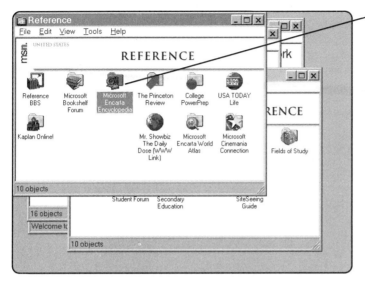

6. Click twice on the **Microsoft Encarta Encyclopedia icon**. The Microsoft Encarta Encyclopedia window will appear.

Notice that there are several other icons that offer online versions of Microsoft's reference products. After you've tried out Encarta, you may want to come back to this window and try the others. The process is almost identical to the one for Encarta.

Note: To read a little about the online version of Encarta before installing it, and to make sure it's not too big to fit on your computer's hard drive, click twice on the Readme First icon and/or the Encarta Intro Edition Features icon.

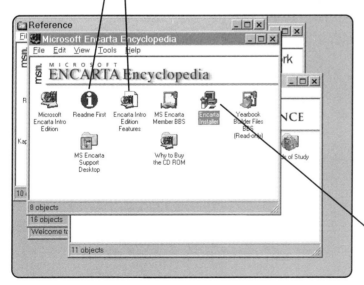

Installing Encarta

Before you can begin using Encarta, you must download a few files. This download will take several minutes (depending on your modem speed), so grab a cup of your favorite beverage and relax!

1. Click twice on the **Encarta Installer icon**. A downloading progress window will appear.

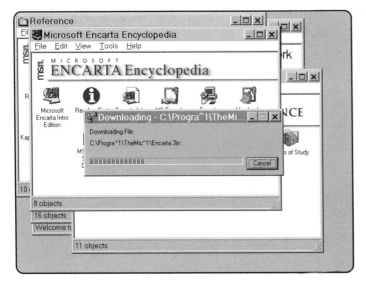

The download process involves the network sending several files to your computer. When all the files have been received, a confirmation dialog box will appear.

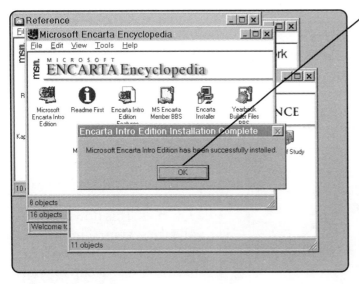

2. **Click** on **OK**. The Microsoft Encarta Encyclopedia window will reappear.

USING ENCARTA

Once you've downloaded the Encarta Intro Edition files, they are ready for use.

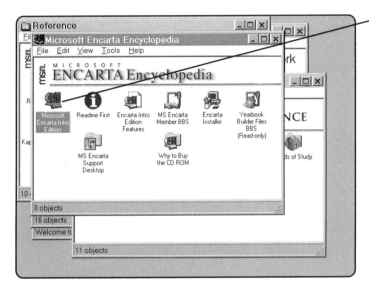

1. **Click twice** on the **Microsoft Encarta Intro Edition icon**. A Microsoft Home dialog box will appear.

Note: You only need to go through the installation process once—each time you come back to this forum from now on you can go right to this step.

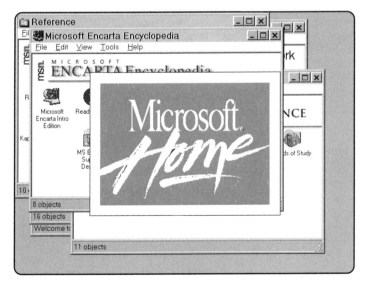

It takes about a minute for Encarta to start up, so be patient. When it's ready, the Encarta opening screen will appear.

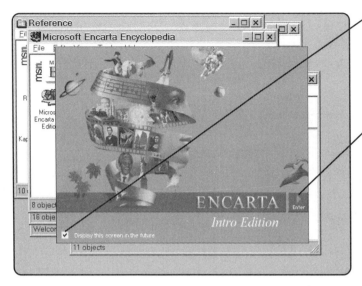

Note: If you want to skip this screen the next time you open Encarta, click on the box at the bottom left of the screen to remove the ✔.

2. **Click** on the **Enter button** at the bottom right of the screen. The MICROSOFT ENCARTA Intro Edition program window will appear.

There are several ways to find information in Encarta. We'll show you the most common way.

3. **Click** on the **Area of Interest button** at the top left of the window. (The name of the current area, Art, Language, & Literature in this example, shows before you click on the button.) A menu will appear.

4. **Move** the **cursor** down to **Life Science**. A category menu will appear.

5. **Click** on **Environment**. The Pinpointer window will appear.

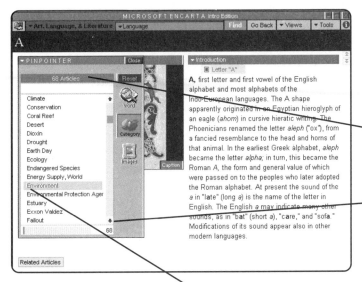

The Pinpointer window helps you do what its name implies—pinpoint the exact article you're looking for within a selected category.

Notice that there are 68 articles within the Environment category.

6. **Scroll down** until Environment comes into view.

7. **Click twice** on **Environment**. The Environment article will appear in the main program window behind the Pinpointer window.

The Pinpointer window remains visible so you can review articles before committing to one. You may also want to explore the Word and Category buttons on the right side of this window to see how you can use them to alter your search. (The Images button will display a list of images available within the category.)

8. **Click** on the **Close button** at the upper right corner of the window. The window will disappear.

Trying the Outline View

Encarta offers different ways to view each article. The outline view lets you quickly navigate through an article.

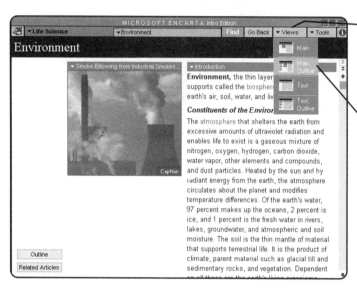

1. **Click** on the **Views button** at the top right of the window. The Views menu will appear.

2. **Click** on **Main, Outline**. The layout of the article will change to include an outline on the left side of the window.

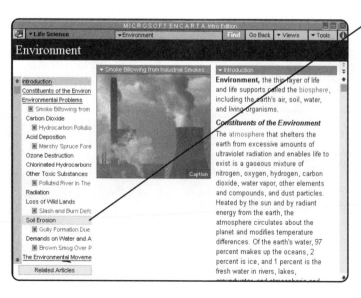

3. **Click twice** on **Soil Erosion** in the outline. The section of the article on soil erosion will be displayed on the right side of the window.

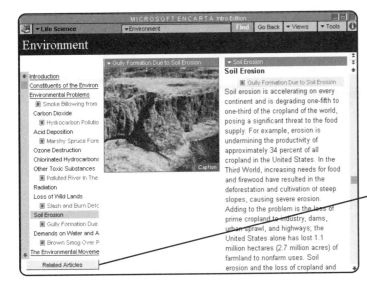

Finding Related Articles

Where appropriate, Encarta also provides a list of related articles so you can explore a topic from different perspectives.

1. **Click** on the **Related Articles button** at the lower left of the window. The Related Articles window will appear.

You can open any article in the list simply by clicking twice on its name.

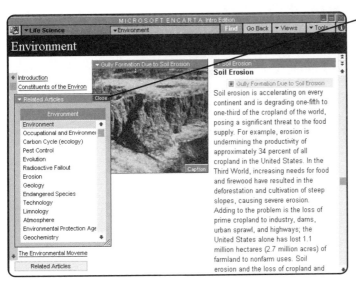

2. **Click** on the **Close button** at the top right of the window. The Related Articles window will disappear.

Printing an Article

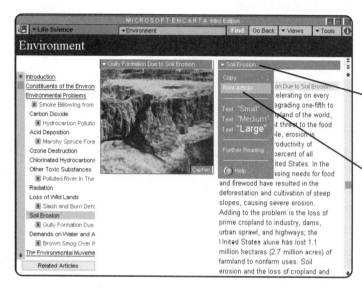

At any time you can print the current article so you have a hard copy version to refer to.

1. Click on the **section title** at the top of the article text. A pop-up menu will appear.

2. Click on **Print Article**. The article will be sent to your printer. (This particular article produced an 8-page report.)

Getting Help

There's a lot more you can do with Encarta that we don't have room to show you here. The program does have a great online help system that makes it easy for you to explore on your own.

1. Click on the **Help icon** at the top right of the window. The Encarta Help window will appear.

To use Encarta's help system, click on a general topic in the left column then click on a specific topic in the middle column. The help for that topic will appear in the right column. Use the right scroll bar to scroll through the information.

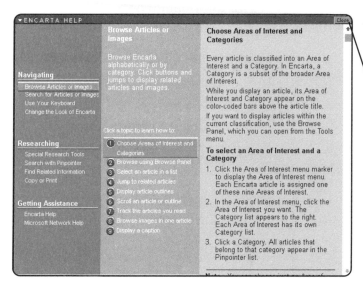

2. When you're finished with the help system, **click** on the **Close button** at the top right of the window.

Quitting Encarta

1. When you're finished with Encarta, **click** on the **Close button** ([X]) on the title bar. The Microsoft Encarta Encyclopedia window will reappear.

SEARCHING MSN FOR A TOPIC

You can also search through all The Microsoft Network services for information on a particular topic using the Find command.

1. Click on **Tools** in the menu bar. The Tools menu will appear.

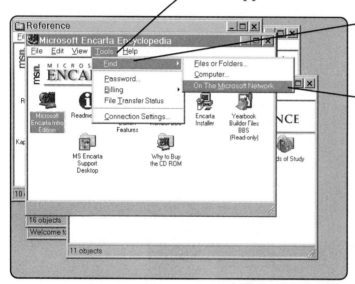

2. Move the **mouse arrow** down to **Find**. A second menu will appear.

3. Click on **On the Microsoft Network**. The Find window will appear.

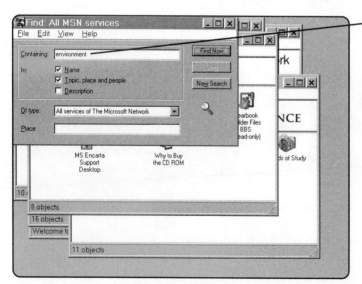

4. Type environment in the Containing box.

5. Press Enter on your keyboard (or click on Find Now). The Find window will expand, and the network will begin its search. When it's finished, the results will be displayed in the lower part of the window.

Checking the Results

As you can see, the search turned up quite a few results (26, as of the day we did our search; the number you get may be different). Let's look at one of them.

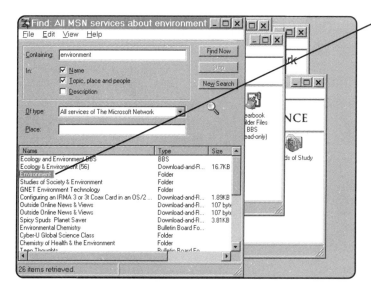

1. **Click twice** on **Environment** in the list at the bottom of the window. The Environment forum window will appear.

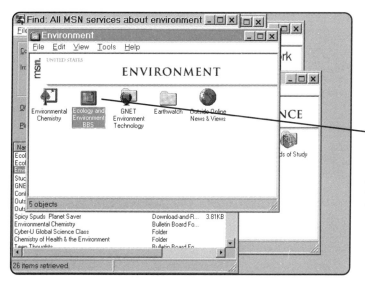

BBSs are great places to do research, because you can ask specific questions and get responses back, often from experts in the field.

2. **Click twice** on the **Ecology and Environment BBS icon**. The Ecology and Environment BBS window will appear.

From this point you can use the skills you learned in Chapter 9 to explore the BBS and post a question or two if you so choose. (You've probably realized by this point that once you master a few basic MSN skills, you can master most of the network.)

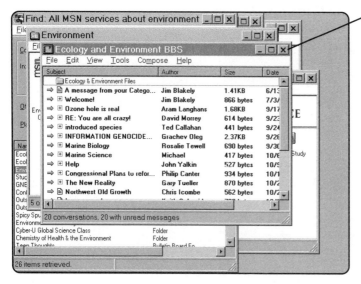

3. When you're finished with the BBS, **click** on the **Close button** ([X]) on the title bar. Repeat this with each window that appears until you are back at the MSN Central window.

Investigating Higher Education Options

If you're preparing for college or graduate school, The Microsoft Network has a special area just for you! In it you'll find everything from advice on selecting a school and finding financial aid to test preparation software. In this chapter, you will do the following:

✔ Find information on colleges from BBSs

✔ Download free test preparation software

GETTING INFORMATION

In this section, you will explore two of MSN's college-oriented areas. You'll also learn where to find other similar areas that you can explore on your own.

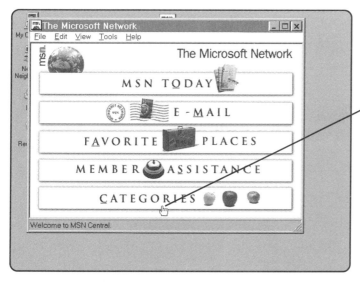

1. **Open The Microsoft Network** to **MSN Central**, if it isn't already on your screen.

2. **Place** the **mouse arrow** on **CATEGORIES**. The arrow will turn into a hand.

3. **Click** on **CATEGORIES**. The Categories window will appear.

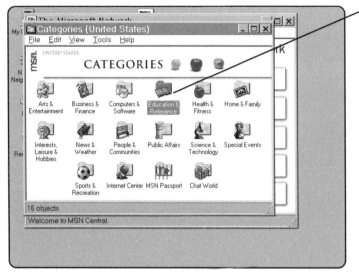

4. Click twice on the **Education & Reference icon**. The Education & Reference window will appear.

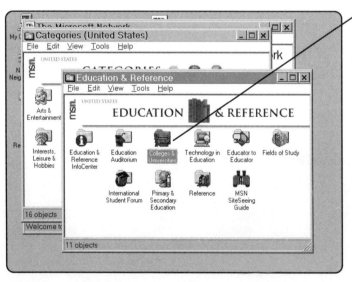

5. Click twice on the **Colleges & Universities icon**. The Colleges & Universities window will appear.

Using the Colleges and Universities BBS

The Colleges and Universities BBS is a great starting place to ask questions and get information.

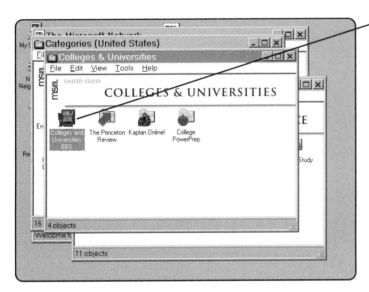

1. **Click twice** on the **Colleges and Universities BBS icon**. The Colleges and Universities BBS window will appear. (See Chapter 9 for details on using BBSs.)

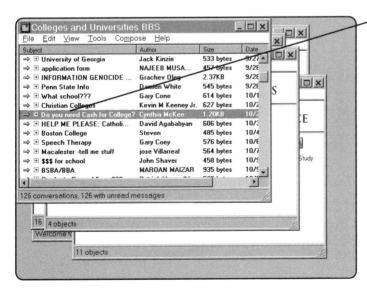

2. **Click twice** on a **topic** that looks interesting to you. A message window will appear.

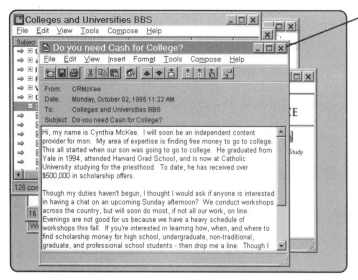

3. When you're finished exploring the BBS, **click** on the **Close button** (⌧) on the title bar. Repeat this with the Colleges and Universities BBS window. The Colleges & Universities window will reappear.

EXPLORING THE PRINCETON REVIEW FORUM

The Princeton Review forum, along with the other forums in this category, offers such resources as advice, sample test questions, and sample test software.

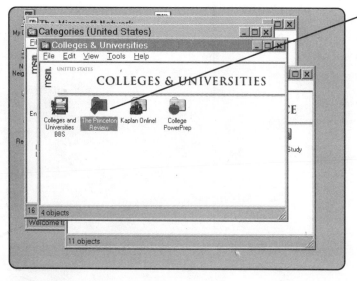

1. Click twice on the **The Princeton Review icon**. The Princeton Review window will appear.

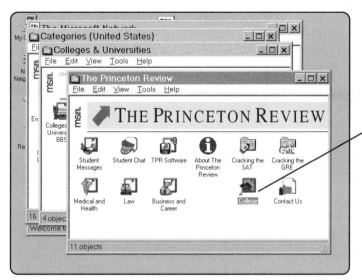

We'll take a quick look at two of the resources The Princeton Review has to offer and let you explore the rest on your own.

2. Click twice on the **College icon**. The College BBS window will appear.

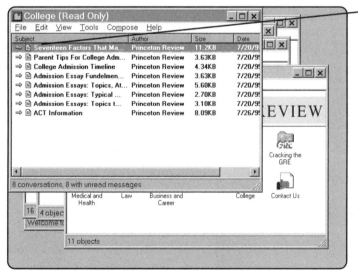

3. Click twice on a **topic** that looks interesting. A message window will appear.

Notice that "(Read Only)" appears in the title bar of this BBS and its corresponding message windows. This means that you cannot add questions to or create new topics in the BBS.

4. Click on the **Close button** ([×]) on the title bar. Repeat this with the College BBS window. The Princeton Review window will reappear.

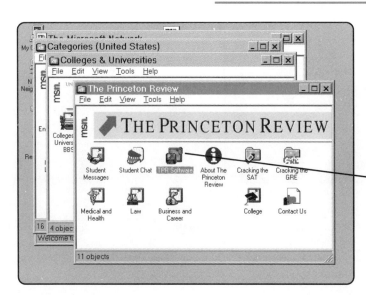

DOWNLOADING TEST PREPARATION SOFTWARE

Each forum in the Colleges & Universities area offers test preparation software of some sort or another. Some of these programs are free, while others carry a nominal charge.

1. Click twice on the **TPR Software icon**. The TPR Software window will appear.

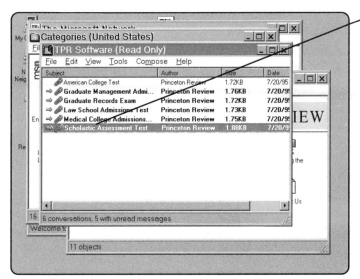

2. Click twice on the **test name** that interests you. A message window will appear.

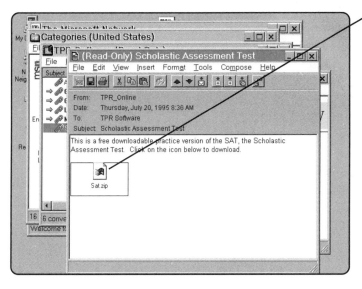

3. Click twice on the **attached document icon**. In this example it's Sat.zip. The Attached File Properties dialog box will appear.

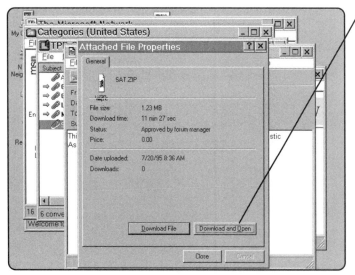

4. **Click** on **Download and Open**. A warning dialog box will appear.

This is a fairly large file that will take a while to download, so the network warns you before sending the file.

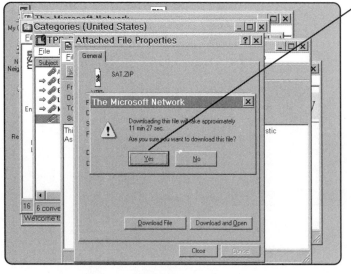

5. **Click** on **Yes**. A down-loading progress dialog box will appear.

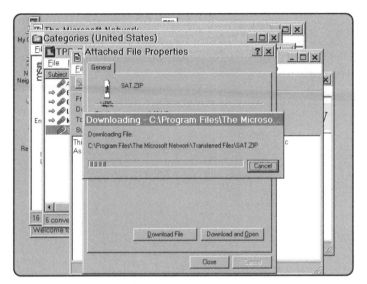

You might as well take a short break at this point while the file downloads. Grab something to eat or review how to use WinZip in Chapter 13.

If you followed along in Chapter 13 and downloaded WinZip, the WinZip order reminder dialog box will appear when the download is complete.

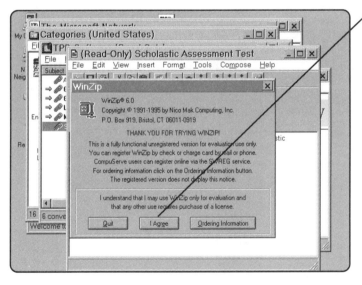

6. **Click** on **I Agree**. The WinZip program window will appear.

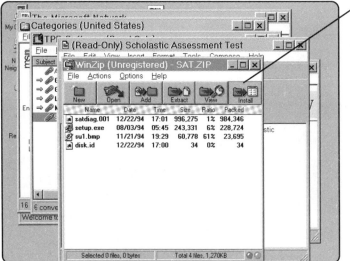

7. Click on the **Install button** at the top right of the window. The Install dialog box will appear.

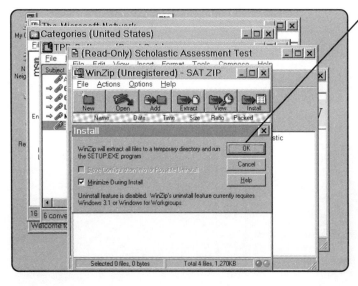

8. Click on **OK**. WinZip will expand the program files and run the install program.

The installation process is very straightforward, so we won't show the rest of the steps here. When it's finished, the Revieware Program Manager window will appear.

At this point you could run the program by clicking twice on the program icon. But since you're still connected to MSN, you'll probably want to do this later.

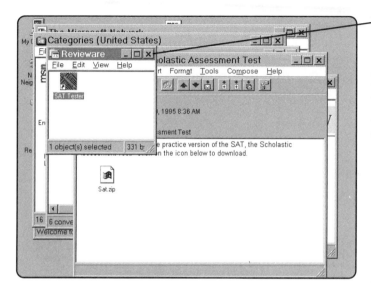

9. When you're finished, **click** on the **Close button** ([X]) on the title bar of the Reviewware window. Repeat this with each window that appears until you are back at the MSN Central window.

Looking for Career Opportunities

If you're looking for a job or considering a career transition, you'll get plenty of help on The Microsoft Network. From sample resumes and cover letters to job listings and networking opportunities, MSN may just give you the extra edge that lands you your next job! In this chapter, you will do the following:

✔ Locate career resources

✔ Review resume styles

✔ Get job search tips

✔ Explore the Career Opportunities BBS

FINDING CAREER RESOURCES

In this section, you will use one of the tools you used in Chapter 15 to locate MSN's career resources.

1. **Open The Microsoft Network** to **MSN Central**, if it isn't already on your screen.

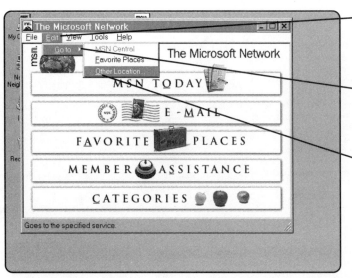

2. **Click** on **Edit** in the menu bar. The Edit menu will appear.

3. **Move** the **mouse arrow** down to **Go to**. A second menu will appear.

4. **Click** on **Other Location**. The Go To Service dialog box will appear.

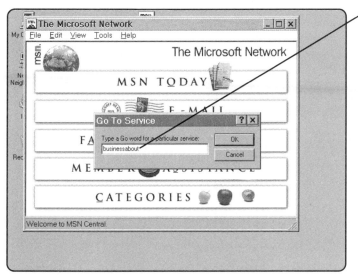

5. Type businessabout in the text box. The network will send the About Business & Finance Category guide to your computer and then open it.

Note: Chapter 6 explains how to find the Go word for a service. Chapter 15 gives details on using the About Business & Finance Category guide.

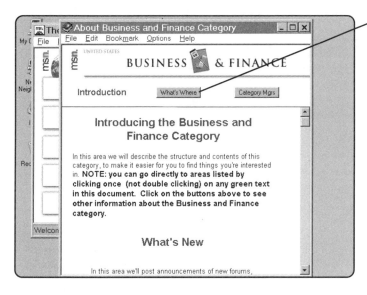

6. Click on the **What's Where button** near the top of the window. The What's Where in Business & Finance page will appear.

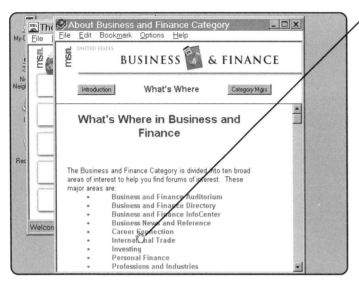

7. **Click** on **Career Connection**. The page will jump to the Career Connection section.

REVIEWING A RESUME STYLE

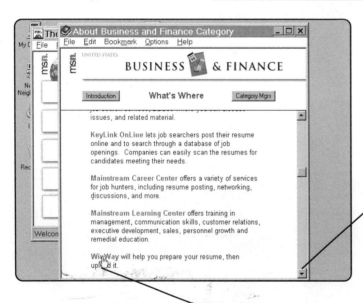

Career Connection gives a handy overview of each of the career resources available on MSN and lets you jump to them with a click of the mouse. In this section, you will use the WinWay Career Forum to review a sample resume style.

1. **Click repeatedly** on the ▼ at the bottom of the right scroll bar until the WinWay description scrolls into view.

2. **Click** on **WinWay**. The WinWay window will appear.

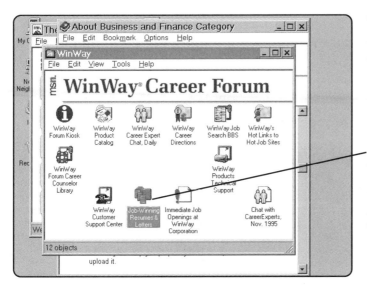

There are several resources to explore in the WinWay Career Forum. We'll look at three of them in this chapter and let you explore the rest on your own.

3. **Click twice** on the **Job-Winning Resumes & Letters icon**. The Job-Winning Resumes & Letters window will appear.

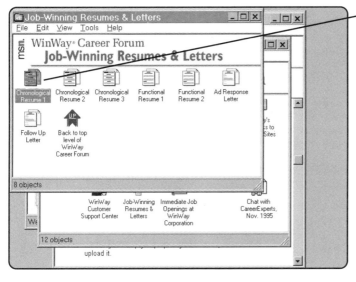

4. **Click twice** on a **document icon** that looks interesting. A document window will appear.

You can scroll through the resume if you like, or click on the Print button at the top left of the window to print a copy.

To find out more about WinWay Resume, the software program that created this resume, click on the More about WinWay Resume 3.0 box.

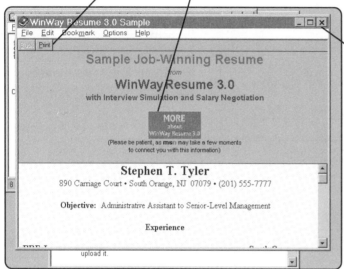

5. **Click** on the **Close button** (⊠) on the title bar. Repeat this with the Job-Winning Resumes & Letters window. The WinWay Career Forum window will reappear.

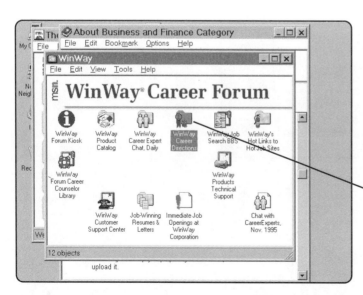

REVIEWING JOB SEARCH TIPS

In this section, you'll use the WinWay Career Forum to review some useful job search tips.

1. **Click twice** on the **WinWay Career Directions icon**. The WinWay Career Directions window will appear.

There are several tips for searching in this area. You'll find each of them to be quite useful, no matter how many jobs you've applied for!

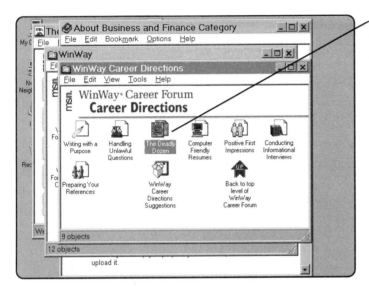

2. **Click twice** on **The Deadly Dozen icon**. A document window will appear.

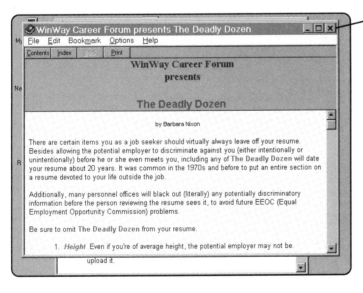

3. When you're done with the document, **click** on the **Close box** (☒) on the title bar. Repeat this with the WinWay Career Directions window. The WinWay Career Forum window will reappear.

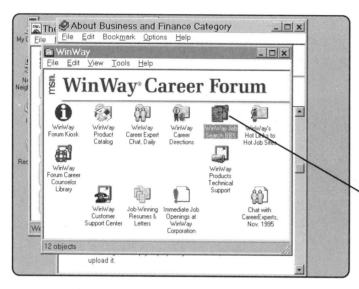

LOOKING AT CAREER OPPORTUNITIES

In this section, you'll take a look at the WinWay Career Forum's Job Search BBS.

1. **Click twice** on the **WinWay Job Search BBS**. The WinWay Job Search BBS window will appear.

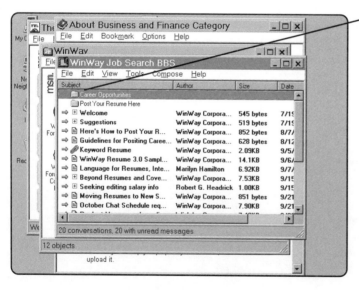

2. **Click twice** on **Career Opportunities**. The Career Opportunities BBS window will appear.

If you see anything that looks interesting, click twice the message title to read the message.

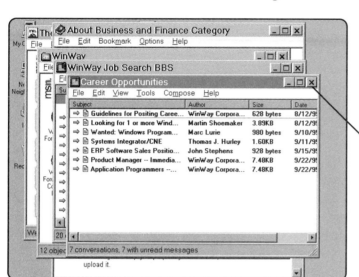

Note: Since job listings change almost constantly, you'll want to come back and check this BBS on a daily basis.

3. **Click** on the **Close button** ([X]) on the title bar. Repeat this with each window that appears until you are back at the About Business and Finance Category window.

Note: At the time this book was written, most of the other Career Connection resources were still under construction. We strongly recommend that you explore each of them on your own. By the time you read this, you should be able to use these resources for such things as searching for specific job openings and uploading your resume for companies to review. Have fun and good luck with your search!

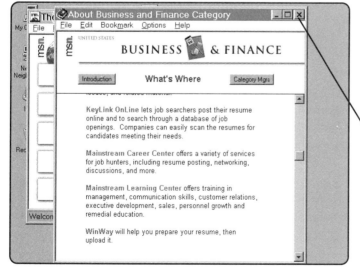

4. When you've finished searching, **click** on the **Close button** ([X]) on the title bar. The MSN Central window will reappear.

The Microsoft Network

Checking Out Internet Explorer

Internet resources that you can use through The Microsoft Network include e-mail, Internet newsgroups, and the World Wide Web (WWW). Chapters 3 and 4 deal with using e-mail, so we won't duplicate that in this chapter. Newsgroups on MSN work almost exactly like MSN BBSs, which were covered in Chapter 9. However, they are open to anyone who has access to the Internet. Internet Explorer is the added Web browser program that lets you use MSN and Windows 95 for access to the WWW. It is available for downloading from MSN. This chapter only shows you where to find Internet Explorer and a little about some other Internet features on MSN. The Internet sources you have access to through MSN are so vast that it would take a separate book to tell you about them all. In this chapter, you will do the following:

✔ Check out some Internet resources on MSN

GETTING INTERNET EXPLORER FROM MSN

You can find Internet resources integrated throughout MSN. However, to make use of them all you need

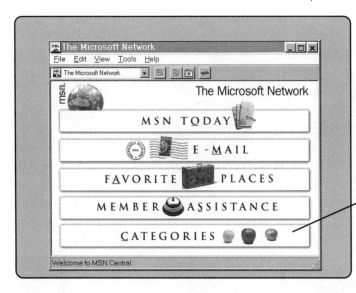

Internet Explorer, the Web browser developed by Microsoft for MSN and Windows 95. We'll start our brief look at the Internet in MSN's Internet Center.

1. **Sign on** to **MSN** if you haven't already done so.

2. **Click** on **Categories**. The Categories window will appear.

You can find links to the Internet in all of the MSN categories. Some are icons that automatically take you to a "Web page." Web pages are what you see when you visit a site, or computer, on the World Wide Web. We'll show you an example of one at the end of this chapter.

Other links to the Internet include icons that take you to Internet Newsgroups, also called Usenet Newsgroups or Newsgroups. On MSN, Internet Newsgroups work just like MSN BBSs. (Review Chapter 9 for details.) The big difference is that only MSN members have access to MSN BBSs, while the whole world has access to Internet Newsgroups.

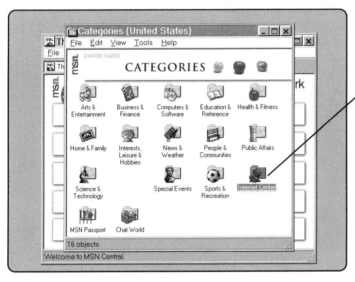

3. **Click twice** on **Internet Center**. The Internet Center window will appear.

Exploring The Internet Center

The Internet Center contains lots of information about the Internet and its use on MSN:

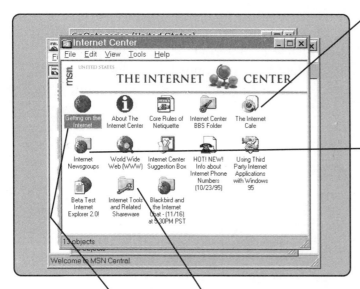

❖ Internet Cafe is a chat area about the Internet. This site and the Internet Center BBS let you exchange information about the Internet with other MSN members.

❖ The Internet Newsgroups icon takes you to folders that list Internet Newsgroups. Review Chapter 2 for details on getting full access to Newsgroups.

❖ There is also a BBS from which you can download Internet Tools (programs for using the Internet).

❖ This category is where you find access to the Internet Explorer software for cruising the Web.

1. **Click twice** on **Getting on the Internet**. This is a download-and-run file, so after a moment, a Downloading message window will appear.

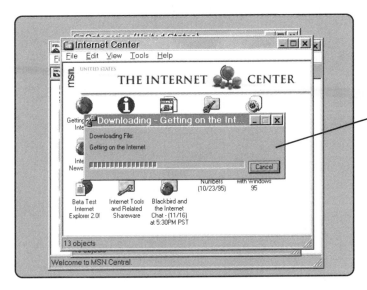

Downloading Internet Explorer

This message window shows the progress of downloading the Getting on the Internet file. Once it's completed, the Getting on the Internet (Overview) window will appear.

The Overview gives you a brief introduction to using the Internet through MSN.

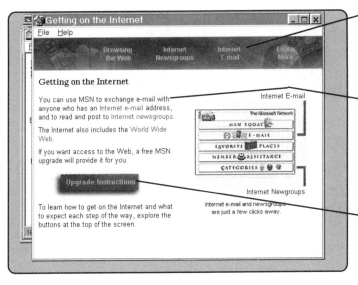

❖ To learn more about e-mail, newsgroups, and the Web, click on the gray text at the top of the window.

❖ Click on the bright blue text for other information.

After exploring these things, come back to the Overview page that you see here.

1. **Click** on **Upgrade Instructions**. The Getting on the Internet (Upgrading...) window will appear.

2. Read the **information** shown here. Note that installation takes at least a half hour, and that you will need your Windows 95 installation CD or disks.

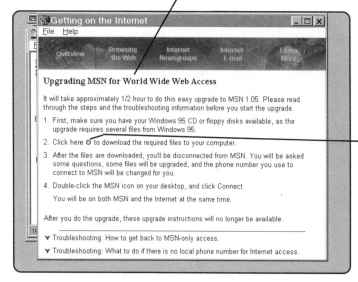

You can come back to Getting on the Internet later if you have problems and need to check the Troubleshooting options at the bottom of this window.

3. Click on the **blue and white star**. The download of the Internet Explorer installation software will begin. Read and follow all of the instructions that you will be given very carefully.

FINDING WEB LINKS

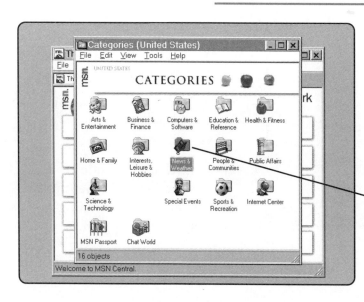

Once Internet Explorer is installed on your computer, you can sign back on to MSN and try some of the links to the Web that can be found throughout the service. We'll show you a favorite of ours, starting back at Categories.

1. Click twice on **News and Weather**. The News and Weather window will appear.

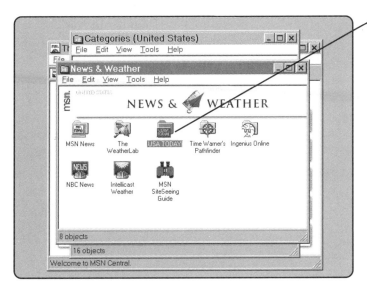

2. Click twice on **USA TODAY**. The USA TODAY window will appear.

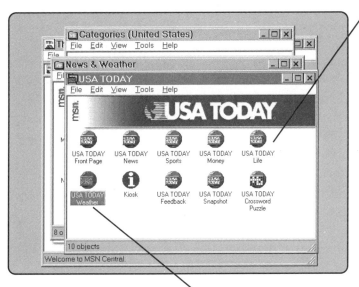

All of the icons in the USA TODAY window include little blue and green globes. This means that they are all links to World Wide Web pages. Whenever you find an icon in MSN that includes one of these globes, it's usually a link to the Web. If you've installed Internet Explorer, you can take a look at our favorite link.

3. Click twice on **USA TODAY Weather**. The Internet Explorer window will appear, and the Web page for USA TODAY Weather will start to load. It will take a few moments for the entire Web page to appear in Explorer.

The USA TODAY Weather Web page gives you a bright, colorful weather map to look at no matter how dismal your weather may be. And there are more links to detailed information about the weather.

The buttons in Explorer's toolbar are used to navigate the Web. Rest your mouse pointer over each one for a moment to see its label. One of the most useful is the globe with a magnifying glass, the third one from the left. This one leads to Web pages where you can search the WWW by subject. Consult online help for more information about using Explorer.

4. **Scroll down** the **page** to see what else is there. You can click on any blue, underlined text to go to yet another Web page.

We hope that you selected the closest, least expensive phone number for connecting to MSN and the Internet. One page can lead to another, then another.... Cruising the Web can be addictive and expensive!

In the introduction to this chapter we mentioned that it would take a whole book to do MSN's Internet resources justice. Well, our completely unbiased recommendation for a very good one is:

Internet for Windows: The Microsoft Network Edition, offered by Prima Publishing, and written by us.

Happy Web surfing!

Part VIII: Appendix

Appendix:	Hiding the Taskbar	Page 266

Hiding the Taskbar

If you do not want the taskbar showing on your screen all of the time, you can hide it from view. This also gives you a little extra screen space for the programs you're using. You can get it back anytime you need it with a simple mouse movement. In this chapter, you will do the following:

✔ Hide the taskbar
✔ Get the hidden taskbar back

REMOVING THE TASKBAR FROM VIEW

1. Click on the **Start button** in the left corner of the taskbar. A menu will appear.

2. Click on **Settings**. Another menu will appear.

3. Click on **Taskbar**. The Taskbar Properties dialog box will appear.

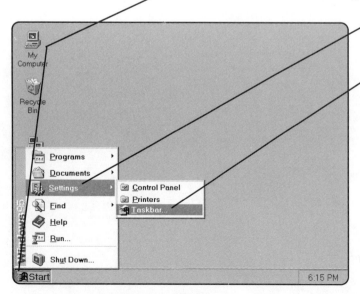

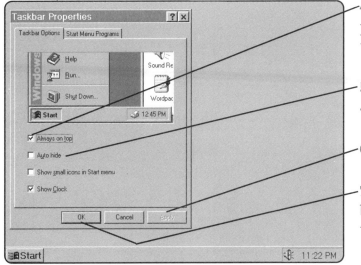

4. **Click** on **Always on top** to put a ✔ in the box if one isn't there already.

5. **Click** on **Auto hide** to put a ✔ in the box.

6. **Click** on **Apply**.

7. **Click** on **OK**. The dialog box will close. The taskbar will disappear in a moment.

GETTING IT BACK

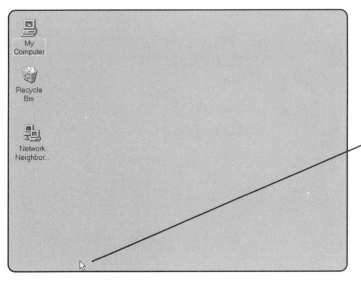

You can get the taskbar back anytime you want it by a simple mouse movement. You can do this at anytime, whether you're running a program or not.

1. **Move** the **mouse pointer** toward the bottom of the desktop.

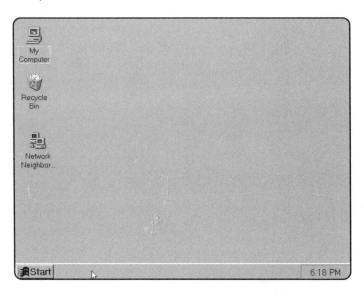

2. **Continue** to **move** the **mouse pointer** until the taskbar reappears.

Note: To hide the taskbar, simply move the mouse pointer away from it.

This works no matter where you've positioned your taskbar, whether at the top, or bottom, or either side of the screen.

Note: If you want to get the taskbar back permanently, repeat steps 1–6 in the first section of this chapter to remove the ✔ from the Auto hide box.

Index

PRIMA'S ALL-TIME **BESTSELLERS!**

Computer Books on the Cutting Edge
PRIMA PUBLISHING

PRIMA PUBLISHING

Computer Professional and Reference

Available Now!

1-2-3 for Windows: The Visual Learning Guide	$19.95
Access 2 for Windows By Example (with 3½-inch disk)	$29.95
Windows Magazine Presents: Access from the Ground Up	$19.95
Access from the Ground Up, 2nd Edition	$19.95
Access for Windows 95: The Visual Learning Guide	$19.95
ACT! 2.0: The Visual Learning Guide	$19.95
Build a Web Site: The Programmer's Guide to Creating, Building, and Maintaining a Web Presence	$34.95
The CD-ROM Revolution	$24.95
CompuServe Information Manager for Windows: The Complete Membership Kit & Handbook (with two 3½-inch disks)	$29.95
Computers Don't Byte	$ 7.95
Computer Gamer's Survival Guide	$19.95
CorelDRAW! 4 Revealed!	$24.95
CorelDRAW! 4 for Windows By Example (with 3½-inch disk)	$34.95
CorelDRAW! 5 Revealed!	$24.95
Create Wealth with Quicken, Second Edition	$19.95
Create Wealth with Quicken, 3rd Edition	$21.95
Cruising America Online 2.5	$21.95
DOS 6.2: Everything You Need to Know	$24.95
Data Security	$34.95
Excel for Windows 95: The Visual Learning Guide	$19.95
Excel 5 for Windows By Example (with 3½-inch disk)	$29.95
Excel 5 for Windows: The Visual Learning Guide	$19.95
Excel for the Mac: The Visual Learning Guide	$19.95
Free Electronic Networks	$24.95
WINDOWS Magazine Presents: Freelance Graphics for Windows: The Art of Presentation	$27.95
Harvard Graphics for Windows: The Art of Presentation	$27.95
IBM Smalltalk Programming for Windows & OS/2 (with 3½-inch disk)	$49.95
Interactive Internet: The Insider's Guide to MUDs, MOOs, and IRC	$19.95
Internet After Hours	$19.95
Internet for Windows: America Online Edition: The Visual Learning Guide	$19.95
Internet for Windows: America Online 2.5 Edition	$19.95
Internet for Windows: The Microsoft Network Edition	$19.95
The Internet Warp Book: Your Complete Guide to Getting Online with OS/2	$21.95
Introduction to Internet Security	$34.95
KidWare: The Parent's Guide to Software for Children	$14.95
Lotus Notes 3 Revealed!	$24.95
LotusWorks 3: Everything You Need to Know	$24.95
Mac Tips and Tricks	$14.95
Macintosh Design to Production: The Definitive Guide	$34.95
Making Movies with Your PC	$24.95
Making Music with Your PC	$19.95
Microsoft Office in Concert	$24.95
Microsoft Office in Concert, Professional Edition	$27.95
Microsoft Works for Windows By Example	$24.95
Migrating to Windows 95	$39.95
OS/2 WARP: Easy Installation Guide	$12.95
PageMaker 4.2 for the Mac: Everything You Need to Know	$19.95
PageMaker 5.0 for the Mac: Everything You Need to Know	$24.95